Renegade Teacher

An Unusual Teacher, A Wily Ol' Superintendent
& The Rebel Kids Who Taught Them So Much

Duane F. Smith

Disclaimer

As anyone who has written about events from the past will tell you, truth is slippery stuff. Events seen from various points of view can become quite different when retold over time. This makes gaining consensus on events which happened in a classroom over 40 years ago not only difficult, but probably impossible. However, every effort has been made by the author to represent the events as accurately as he remembers them, and someone had to write this story. So, I will take responsibility for this, my version of how it all happened.

If you were part of this story and any part of it is not the way you remember it, I apologize and acknowledge that your memory of what happened will be just as valid as mine. Maybe, in some cases, even more so. Furthermore, I encourage you to write me telling me of your version of the event in question, sending it to me in care of the publisher. I would love to hear from you.

The names of the people involved have been changed to protect the privacy of the individual unless, in a few cases, they gave me their explicit permission to use their names.

The Author

Copyright © 2012, Duane F. Smith

All rights reserved

No part of this book may be reproduced in any form without the permission in writing from the publisher. Inquiries should be addressed to:

Ashland Press
2165 West Jackson Road
Ashland OR 97520

A Tribute to Teachers Everywhere

This book is dedicated to teachers everywhere who do a superb job of Educating the majority of our kids, often working under difficult conditions for inadequate pay; doing the best they can, with what they have.

This is a story of an experimental classroom where for, 5 years, a superintendent and teacher threw out the curriculum, and turned everything upside down. Then, they invited the kids who were failing despite the other teachers best efforts. Then, they added some troublemakers and some bright but bored kids. The kids all set their own pace and chose their own areas of interest. This is the surprising story of what worked and what didn't.

Dedicated To

The kids from whom we learned so much and to Henry O. Pete, the most innovative educator I ever met, who gave so many, so much.

A special thanks to Dave and Joan Vokac, authors of The Great Towns of America *Book Series; Joan for her technical expertise and both for convincing me the story was worth telling, and indeed, needed to be heard.*

Thanks to my ever suffering editors, MaryAlice Smith and Peggy Mitchell, who cheerfully edit behind a dyslexic and always keep their good humor.

What the Kids, As Adults, Now Say About Their Program

———— • ————

When I got to Mr. Smith's sixth grade, I thought everything was impossible for me. By the end of that year, I thought nothing was. That was the only year I liked school and learned much of what I use in my business today.

Randy McCarty, Owner
Randy's Plumbing and Heating Contractors, Inc., Medford, Oregon

———— • ————

Mr. Smith was so inspiring and so outside-the-box. He taught us how to think and create, hands-on. He gave us the confidence in that grade to believe we could do anything and achieve what we wanted in life.

Jan Hooks, Owner
Jan Hooks Real Estate Group, Freeport, Florida

———— • ————

I'll never forget Mr. Smith; always thinking outside-the-box. We always were doing another project and always making it work. I can count on one hand the people who helped so much down that long road. I'll always remember that year with Mr. Smith; raising the mice, the crystal radios and the egg cartons. They are all still in my mind. Thanks Duane.

Scott Sutherland Woods
Truck Manager at Biomass One, White City, Oregon

———— • ————

After nearly 16 years of education, it is curious that the most memorable year of school was my sixth grade class with Duane. That year an adult came into my life who was secure enough in himself to treat me as an equal, no hierarchy of teacher/student, just two individuals sharing and relating. 40 years later, nothing has changed and he is still part of my life.

Mark Tolstoy, Executive Chef
Whispering Pines Retirement Community, Redmond, Oregon

———— • ————

He expanded our minds. He opened the door to a huge world. It wasn't just little Phoenix, Oregon anymore.

Dennis Hurd, Owner
B&D Gutters, Medford Oregon

———— • ————

I was bored in school before. He made learning fun and more hands on. It was a very special time in my life.

Scott Wolf, Owner
Rogue Mechanical Insulation, Medford, Oregon

CONTENTS

1. The Flock Returns to the Nest 1
2. How it all Began 3
3. Into the Lion's Den 9
4. Mr. Smith's Class Meets Ma Bell 13
5. The Cast of Characters 17
6. An Unreachable Girl Shows Up 23
7. A Key Technique 27
8. The Crystal Radio Affair 31
9. Bobby James Smith 35
10. The Crystal Radio Goes Entrepreneurial 41
11. Crack Shows—or Does It? 49
12. The Mouse Farm Enterprise 53
13. Billy Johnson and his Whiskey Bottles 61
14. The Grim Reaper Visits Mousedom 63
15. The Boy and the Box of Golden Oak 67
16. Ronnie Crosses the Big Divide 73
17. Grades 1 Through 12 in 90 Days? 77
18. Teresa Tries It Again 83
19. The Inquisition 85
20. Teaching Problem Solving 89
21. Chess Ladder and State Tournament 95
22. Teresa Moves On 97
23. The Itinerant Flute Maker 103
24. The Impossible Saltwater Aquarium 107
25. The Worst Speller in the Class 109
26. You Win Some 113
27. Life, Death and the Sears Catalog 117
28. Henry Turns Cryptic and I Take Stock 123
29. Henry Reveals All 125
30. The Life Changing Decision 123
31. Scattering to the Four Winds 125
32. Jan's Call from Florida 131
ABOUT THE AUTHOR 137

Chapter 1

The Flock Returns to the Nest

Maybe you can never return home after you left the nest but sometimes you can find the old neighborhood.

It's not often we can return to some nostalgic part of our past; back to a time and place gone forever, along with the Beatles and 25-cent coffee; back to sights and sounds still lingering somewhere in some dim, 3rd story attic of our minds. However, I did so not long ago. Feelings of déjà vu flooded over me as I seemingly walked into a classroom where I had taught a most unusual group of kids in an old building I knew was long gone.

The kids were there, although older and grayer, but I recognized most of them. Of course, part of my mind knew I was really at a country inn in Ashland, Oregon, and it was 40 years later. However, some way, those "kids" had magically transformed part of this inn back into the old classroom where we had all been together so long ago. Also with me that night was Henry, the wily ol' superintendent who had brought us all together and changed all our lives forever, including his.

The room was even the same, with old worn-out sofas and mismatched carpeting, an old-fashioned blackboard, work tables covered with old radio parts and crystal radios the kids had built themselves.

Renegade Teacher

In addition, the walls and ceiling were covered with egg cartons, just as they had been back then.

At this point one of the "kids" escorted Henry and me to our special seats for what they were calling their "40 Year Reunion with 'Smith'," and I was beginning to feel a bit like I was on the old 1950s television show, "This is Your Life." And, as I sat waiting for the festivities to begin, I couldn't help but reflect back to the day it all started over 40 years ago.

Chapter 2

How it all Began

*A firing at work can sometimes be a relief,
even if you are the one being fired.*

It had been a cold wintry day in December. The class and I were safe inside, going about a normal day in our offbeat classroom. I was sitting on an old, worn piece of carpet strewn on the wooden floor, surrounded by a ragtag bunch of kids when Wesley, the principal, walked into my classroom. Close behind him was a tall balding man I knew to be the superintendent. Wesley had finally called in the big guns; my goose was cooked, and I knew this meant the end of my short tenure as a teacher at Phoenix Elementary School in rural southern Oregon. In some ways it didn't matter, but I couldn't help wondering what would happen to the kids in my class, some who were just about at the end of their short ropes.

It had started out as a normal enough day in my fifth grade classroom. The Beatles were playing *Love Me Do* on an old stereo some kid had cobbled together and the smell of popcorn saturated the air. A tousle-haired boy was digging through a beat-up old refrigerator that looked right at home amid an odd assortment of old sofas and mismatched furniture. Two boys had the guts of an old tube radio spread across the floor, probably salvaging parts for something they were building.

As for me, I was reading to a group of kids as we sprawled on the

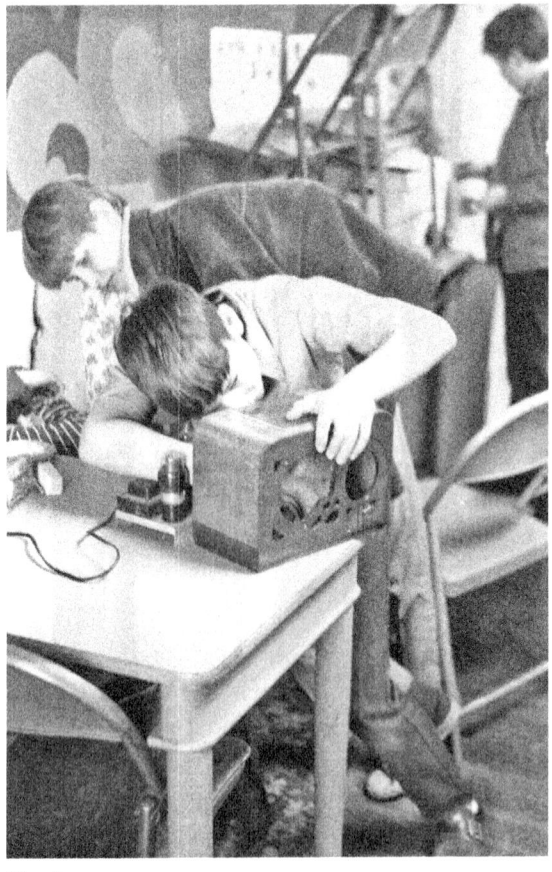

The doctor operates.

floor, most propped up on some old sofa cushions. The cushions were scattered about on the worn carpet in front of a particularly shabby-looking old sofa with stuffing coming out of its arms. There weren't any school desks. We got rid of them the first few weeks of school to make room for more important things. All in all, the furnishings lent an air of shabbiness to the room, but the kids didn't seem to mind.

I guess it wasn't hard to understand why Wesley was at his wit's end. The general disarray was probably what he objected to even more than the shabbiness, other than perhaps my calling him Wesley instead of Mr. Worthington. With Wesley, decorum and order ranked right up there next to godliness. Of course, there also was the matter of my necktie, which was usually gone by the time school started. In my style of hurly-burly teaching, I moved around too much to be constrained by a tie. In Wesley's world, a teacher lost the respect of parents and pupils when he didn't wear a tie.

So you can see the problem. I didn't fit Wesley's picture of a proper grade school teacher, what his room should look like, how it should operate and how he should dress. And it looked like he was finally going to do something about it, and it was about time; I was tired of the tension.

One of the girls fixing something.

I had seen it coming for some time now. A couple of weeks earlier, I was called to Wesley's office over a matter of gum chewing. At the beginning of the year, while we still had desks, the subject of gum chewing came up in the teachers' room. It seemed to really offend a few of the other teachers that I allowed it in my classroom.

I allowed it because one day in class, one of the boys asked why gum chewing wasn't allowed. I told them to look under the desks and tell me what they saw. Chewing gum galore, they reported. So I told them that was the reason.

"Yeah, but...Smith!"—I got that a lot from my class, "Yeah, but" and "Smith"—"we just stick it there because we can't put it in the trash can or we would get caught." I had no comeback for that one, so we struck a deal. They would remove all the old gum currently on the desks and furniture. In return, they would be allowed to chew gum in the future as long as all of it went into the trash can when they had worn it out, and not on the floor or in someone's hair. As long as that happened, gum chewing was okay in Mr. Smith's room. However, if one piece of gum ever ended up in an untoward place, it would once again be banned from the room.

In short order, Wesley had me in his office. He patiently explained how it was disrespectful for children to chew gum in school. When I told him I thought respect was something earned by the teacher, not

Work space was where you could get it.

received by forbidding them to chew gum, he fell back to the old line of it being against the rules at Phoenix Elementary School.

Then I made another of my many unpardonable comebacks. "Really, Wesley," I said, "I don't seem to remember gum chewing being mentioned in the student handbook," as I picked up his copy of the Phoenix Elementary Rule Book off his desk where it was always handy. Of course I did that so he couldn't. However, he recovered quickly by reaching inside his desk and pulling out his backup copy, immediately starting to go through it. But I knew I had him because gum chewing wasn't mentioned in his rule book. I know, I had already looked carefully. After going through it three times, he finally said, "Well, I guess it got overlooked."

So my kids disrespectfully chewed gum, popped popcorn, made and ate sandwiches, made and drank lemonade, listened to the Beatles and played chess by the hour as they did assignments, wrote stories, read books and learned about the world. Needless to say, it drove the kids in other classrooms nuts, and that did not engender love between me and some of the other teachers.

Soon enough, Wesley made it clear in no uncertain terms that changes had to be made in my fifth grade classroom. Poor Wesley's hair was falling out in patches. He was developing large bald spots on the side of his head which I understood were stress related; and without a doubt both my classroom and I were some of the biggest stresses in Wesley's life. I had to go.

Not surprisingly, one morning a few days later, Wesley and the superintendent waltzed through my classroom door. I stayed where I was sitting on the carpet since it wouldn't have made any difference anyway. I continued to read to my small group of kids, who were oblivious to what was about to happen. We were at a "sweet spot" in the story, as the kids called all the good parts, and nothing else mattered.

Wesley strode smugly around the room with Henry (heck, I probably wasn't even supposed to know Henry's first name, let alone refer to him that way) lagging along behind. As they walked around the room, I noticed a small wry, bemused grin on Henry's face. This man was going to relish what he was about to do.

As Henry came around the room and got to where I was still reading on the floor, he paused a minute and then squatted down beside me saying, "Could you come over to my office after school?" Without looking up, I said, "Sure." Without another word, Henry and Wesley left.

The afternoon slipped by slowly. In some ways, what was going to happen was a relief since I already had a construction company to run. It probably had been a bad idea to take the job of teaching for the winter anyway, and most of my kids would probably continue to muddle through as they had before. But, the question remained: What about the other kids?

"Smith" and one of the braver other teachers.

Chapter 3

Into the Lion's Den

For want of a nail the shoe was lost. For want of a shoe the horse was lost. For want of a horse the rider was lost. For want of a rider the battle was lost. For want of a battle the kingdom was lost. And all for the want of a horseshoe nail. Would having known that made the horseshoe nail feel better?

After school I packed up the few things I would take with me; some mementoes of the kids, a few pictures, but not much else. Wesley could have the three old sofas, the old carpet, the miscellaneous old radios, the old sewing machine and the refrigerator. Somehow I got perverse pleasure thinking about Wesley having to deal with all that worn-out junk I had dragged in from a nearby auction barn.

Like a condemned man, I entered Henry's lair. Even if one is ready to leave, it is never fun to be fired. His secretary eyed me as she spoke into the intercom. Then she gestured down the hall. I took that to mean I was to walk the last mile alone.

Henry met me at the door and motioned for me to sit in front of his desk as he took a seat on the other side in his oversized chair. Being important, I guess, he needed a big chair. He sat there and just looked at me for a few minutes as if he wasn't sure exactly how to proceed.

After a while he threw me a curve and said, "What are you going to do next year?" This being just before Christmas, I assumed he meant in January, after he fired me. "Well," I said, "I own some apartments and a small construction company, so I will go back and build some more apartments."

He looked at me some more. I wanted to say, "Come on, let's get on with this. Fire me and get it over with." Instead I waited and he finally said, "If you could do anything you wanted with a classroom of kids, what would you do?"

I didn't know where he was going with that question, but it didn't sound too promising. I assumed he was talking about my unorthodox approach to teaching and not about subject matter. Tentatively I said, "You mean with a class?" He nodded and I jumped in. At least I would get in a few jabs on the way out the door.

You see, as a student in a public school, I hadn't done well. I had been what later would be labeled as dyslexic and barely got through school, graduating in the bottom third of my high school class. I went to college for a short spell because that's what you were supposed to do in my family.

In my branch of the Smith clan, the prevailing culture was to either work or attend school. There were no alternatives, as I had come from a long line of English, Scottish and Irish hellfire and brimstone preachers or orthodox schoolteachers. The Protestant work ethic was well entrenched within the Smith lineage. After the second time I was kicked out of college, Dad refused to help me be readmitted, saying maybe I should join the Army and grow up.

Because of my dyslexia, the entire educational process for me was a time of anger, frustration and then rebellion. At the time I did what every kid does; I blamed myself for all my failures. I was the one out of step. Nothing ever occurred to me other than that I was dumb and lazy. I never suspected that the school wasn't "meeting my needs" as they later would call it. It wasn't until years later that I got even a clue to anything different.

I had a lot of heat built up around the topic of teachers, schools and how they operated and I let Henry have it with both barrels. For the next 25 to 30 minutes, I went on about all the things I believed kids could be doing, indeed should be doing, in school instead of what they were doing now.

As Henry sat there with a bemused, enigmatic smile, there was no stopping me. I was on a roll. I had waited a long time to tell a teacher-type person what side of the toast the butter was on and I was going to make the most of it. I had never before even landed a teacher for my tirade, but now I had a superintendent. I was unstoppable.

Henry let me rant on, and when I finally stopped he just sat there looking at me with that damned enigmatic smile. After what seemed to be several minutes, he just said, "You got it." Then it was my turn to just sit there. I had no idea where this conversation had gone, but it had definitely left me behind. "I got what?" I asked, a bit bewildered. Henry looked at me as though he were a patient man dealing with a slow child and said, "If you come back next year you can have a class of kids with which you can do all those things."

I looked for flecks of foam around the corners of the man's mouth. Nothing he said made any sense, and I was scrambling to get a perch on where this was all going. He could see the bewilderment on my face so he simply said, "If you will come back next fall, you can have a class of kids you can work with in any way you want." Then he went on to say, "But there is a caveat; you'll have to take the kids no one else wants. You'll get the three kids out of each of the fourth, fifth and sixth grade classrooms that the teachers think are holding back their classes. Some may be bright but bored, some will be troublemakers, and some are just kids the teachers have given up on. That way the other teachers won't care what you do with them in your class."

I was scrambling mentally to get my head around the direction this conversation had taken. I had come to the chopping block and he was talking about next year. Good grief, what had I gotten myself into? I had only planned to teach one year and just stir the pot a little. Now he was suddenly talking a whole new ball game. I mentally checked the calendar to see if it was April Fool's Day. Nope, still December.

So that afternoon, in the process of getting fired, I met the man who was to change all our lives. However, at the time, I had no idea that I was in for a lifetime commitment. I had just been given a chance to prove what I had come to believe about the role of school in the life of a child. Would it be possible to really help children learn about life, instead of trying to teach them subject matter.

Chapter 4

Mr. Smith's Class Meets Ma Bell

I always thought it strange that schools designed to teach kids about the world outside shut them in a classroom eight hours a day, with few ways of communicating with the world they are learning about.

The next year, true to his word, Henry gave me a motley crew of about 30 kids. Some were bright, but bored; some were already failing in life and some were just troublemakers. My job was to first see if we could change their general direction; second, to hopefully instill in them some of the skills needed to survive in a rapidly changing future.

To be successful with these ambitious goals, we would need more than currently available methods and textbooks, all of which just contained facts and data about history. Traditional methods had already failed on this bunch. Also, weren't the facts and data in our textbooks and curriculum all about the past? Wasn't that going in the wrong direction if we were to teach about the future? However, after all the head scratching, it left us with an age-old dilemma, how do we prepare kids for a future none of us can predict?

As we followed this fragile trail of logic to a dead end, it grew increasingly clear we needed to be teaching life skills and techniques, not just content and data. Perhaps we could give these kids the ability to successfully navigate the twists and turns of the future as it unfolded ahead of them. After all, we drive a car by looking out of the front window and reacting to what appears, not by looking out the rear window and remembering the pothole and bumps our driving instructor taught us about. Maybe we could at least give these kids great driving skills, instead of just facts and figures about what the old road looked like.

It seemed we needed to teach skills like information gathering, communication, critical thinking and problem solving. However, once again, how do we do that? Well, one thing did seem clear. I didn't know about other classrooms, but the kids in this class had a thousand questions about the world around them, questions I didn't know the answers to. So, the first thing on the agenda was to solve that delema.

My first stop was the Red Barn Auction, down the road a couple of miles from the school, where for $15 I got my first "window to the world," an old television set with rabbit ears. The next step was a little trickier, but since I ascribed to the Jesuit rule for getting things done (it's easier to ask forgiveness than permission), I called Ma Bell and asked to have a telephone installed in my classroom. This was in a district with only one phone in the administration building and one phone in each of its schools. The phone in our school was in the principal's office and that phone was (enter commanding deep voice and add drum-roll, please) "for official business only."

At first I thought the telephone company's bureaucracy was going to thwart my plans. "No, I don't have the principal's authorization, and no, I don't have the school district's permission either." But when I reminded them that schools are public property and I was part of that public and that I would be responsible for paying the bill myself, Ma Bell soon showed up to install a phone in my classroom. By lunchtime that next day, Smith's class was connected to the outside world with both a phone and a television set.

Now, you wouldn't believe the ruckus this started. About the time the phone was operable, I was in the principal's office being asked to explain what was going on in my classroom.

"You mean the telephone? Oh that! Well yes, I had a telephone installed in my classroom," I replied. Wesley looked at me like I was an addled child and started to flush a little in the face. He took a deep breath and seemed unsure what rule in his rule book this came under, because apparently it hadn't come up before. Then he got a bit of a grip on himself and patiently explained that telephones aren't permitted in the classrooms at Phoenix Elementary School.

When I asked why, he replied, "For budgetary reasons." So then I explained that I had taken responsibility for the phone bill. Still, no dice. So then I used my line which had worked so well with the phone company, the one on how the school was public property and how I was a member of the public and was paying the bill myself. But the fact that I was paying the bill for a phone on public property didn't seem to ease his mind one bit. He insisted I take the phone out immediately, and with that I was told that I was free to go.

However, I always was a bit of a procrastinator, and very soon Wesley told me I was to appear in front of the school board to explain my insubordination. Of course Henry was the moderator of school board meetings, but it was early in our relationship so I had no idea how this was going to fly, but in some way I felt it would.

Luckily, just a few days before the monthly school board meeting, a very fortuitous event occurred in the skies over Phoenix, Oregon. We had a UFO (in the sense that no one knew what the object was) hover directly overhead for a day or two. Visible to the naked eye at high altitude, it produced a lot of speculation in the local press. As it turned out, the local newspaper discovered that Mr. Smith's class at Phoenix Elementary School knew more about the UFO than anyone in the valley.

The kids had inaugurated the lines of the new telephone with repeated calls seeking an explanation of the UFO, finally reaching the Lyndon B. Johnson Space Center in Houston, Texas. After repeated grilling by a group of fifth and sixth graders, the Space Center eventually explained how it would be gone as soon as the weather patterns changed.

This episode preceded my summons to appear in front of the school board, and I spent nearly an hour explaining how the kids went about tracking down who was behind the UFO. Plus I did plenty of espousing on my theories of how kids need to interact with the outside world if they were to learn more than just Readin', Writin' and 'Rithmetic and the insides of their little room at Phoenix Elementary School. I also went on to explain how, if approached correctly, they would learn a lot about the 3 R's in the process of doing exciting things. The board seemed open-minded and soon was asking dozen of questions. Wesley, of course, was in attendance, and I thought I could see his stress levels go up measurably that evening.

Permission for keeping the phone was granted unanimously, and soon the phone an intregal part of our learning apparatus. Now if the students had a question about anything (and thirty inquiring minds had dozens of questions every day) we first talked over where they might find some answers and planned the questions they were going to ask. After picking a designated "phoner," and with plan in hand, they fired away. They talked locally to building officials, health inspectors, lawyers, and doctors, as well as to experts from the Space Center in Houston, again and again. To the credit of the staff there, they never seemed to tire of the questions about space-related things and who-knows-what-else they were asked.

It was a truly amazing experience for me, watching them grow in their understanding of the world and about life in the rest of America, far away from their little town of 3,500 people in rural southern Oregon. Also, the responsibility for the telephone bill kept the class on the lookout for ways to make extra money to pay for it. Partly out of the need to pay that bill, they baked cookies and set up a sales booth for selling popcorn and lemonade to the other students during recess time and after school. The telephone had broadened their minds in even more ways than I'd originally dreamed.

Chapter 5

The Cast of Characters

It is difficult for one maverick to be effective in an organization. However, two mavericks work well in a school, as long as the second is the Superintendent.

The Teacher

The Teacher was a misfit in school himself. He was born with what is now known as dyslexia at a time when little was known about the condition or the negative effect it could have in the learning process. In school, he struggled with the challenges we now associate with the condition. Worse than the dyslexia were the labels teachers pinned on him because of the difficulties it caused him. During that period, he was to hear his teachers tell his parents over and over again, "Duane is capable of far better work; he just doesn't apply himself."

One high school counselor even told his distressed mother after three days of vocational testing, "Duane would make an excellent butter wrapper," in the days when butter was still wrapped by hand. Being an ex-teacher herself, this didn't go down well with her because she, as a mother, expected great things from her son. Still, she had a good sense of humor and took it in stride.

As he moved through the primary grades, his frustrations grew along with his temper. In the fifth grade, he was to meet a teacher who was a real life changer, but in a negative way. He remembers her as a self-righteous, frustrated woman who thought the way to motivate children, little boys in particular, was to shame them into better performance. Her way of inspiring and motivating a student was to hold up their work in front of the class, ridicule it and then post it on a special bulletin board for all to examine. If her efforts created a negative reaction, she would only increase the pressure. In Duane's case, instead of motivation, it created shame, anger and rebellion.

With his above-average IQ and good reading and verbal skills, he was passed on through the grades into high school, even though he was functionally illiterate in writing, spelling and grammar. In high school, the results of his written work were much the same. Classes that required writing, spelling and grammar continued to be extremely frustrating. In math, science and physics he did well, and would usually receive As and Bs for his work if the teacher wasn't big on homework. He still had an attitude problem and refused to do anything outside of class. Classes where he could rely on his verbal skills went reasonably well, so he managed to graduate on time but in the lower third of his class.

After a short stint in college, his lack of writing skills and study habits, along with his partying, finally caught up with him. By this time his father realized the futility of getting him reinstated in college each time he was kicked out. He suggested that his son go into the Army and grow up. The Army appealed to the boy's sense of adventure and so, to everyone's great relief, he agreed to "Join the Army and See the World," as a recruiting slogan at that time said. He left for the Army feeling like he had a big "D" for "Dumb" branded across his forehead.

After his basic training, he was shipped to Europe for his tour of duty. He quickly learned to play the Army game well enough to rise in rank, to the point that he always had a three-day pass in his pocket for weekends. With the weekends, added to the ninety days of leave-time received for his 3 years enlistment, all of Europe beckoned. He would buy a succession of old Volkswagens and ancient Mercedes which were a dime a dozen in Germany at the time and with transportation at hand, he set out to explore the nooks and crannies of Europe.

Ninety thousand miles on the back roads of Europe just a decade or so after World War II was to influence him for the rest of his life. American money in Europe was a highly desirable commodity then. German beer was the equivalent of 15 cents a liter, gasoline 19 cents a gallon, a great wienerschnitzel dinner was three or four German Marks, and a night in a 300-year-old Gasthaus was about $3. He was particularly fond of the small inns that graced the forests and back roads; they planted the seeds that would lead to his building the European-style country inn later in Ashland, Oregon, after he left teaching. He found people everywhere in Europe extremely friendly, and in a number of cases he formed lifelong friendships.

His three-year tour of duty went by quickly; but as he was approaching his European departure date, the Berlin Crisis flared up and his tour of duty was extended six months. This created another life-changing event. During this extension period, he met a cute fraulein and her strict German mother. He was smitten. Six months later, as his new Army discharge date approached, he was denied his application to be discharged in Germany. So with a heavy heart, he shipped the new Volkswagen he had just bought back to New York and boarded a troopship, leaving his sweetheart behind. After being discharged in New York, he spent a month meandering across the country on his way back home to Oregon.

After six months at home, he sorely missed the European way of life and his little fraulein. So he sold his new Volkswagen and headed back to Germany. Her strict mother soon consented to their marriage. To support his new bride he began exporting a model of Volkswagen into the US market that wasn't available there at the time. Life was good, great wine was cheap and the young couple was in love. It seemed that the good times would last forever. But, it was not to be.

Volkswagen International decided to export into the United States the same model Duane was making his living sending back to America, so the couple packed up and set out for his hometown in Oregon. Once again, after docking in New York and picking up their old Mercedes at the dock, he set out on another month-long odyssey across America, this time with a new bride. They had $17.50 to their name after filling up in New York, but both were good workers and they would stop and work along the way as needed. After all, they were young and in love; the world was golden and this was all just their first big adventure together. And, after a month or so, once again he rolled up to the ranch, this time with his wife.

At first, he tried his hand at selling cars, but still found himself avoiding people and circles where he might have to interact with people who seemed "educated." But, soon he began to hear the voice of his parents ringing somewhere in his head. "You must finish college." Finally, the couple moved to Ashland, Oregon where they could at least be closer to a college. After working at an automobile dealership for a while, he started remodeling old houses, while trying to screw up courage enough to face his worst fears.

Because he knew he hadn't paid attention to anything school-wise since the fifth grade, he prepared himself with the knowledge that college would be extremely difficult. But he was determined to persevere and finish with a degree, no matter what it took.

To his utter amazement college proved to be a breeze. This left him wondering how this could be. Why did he suddenly seem to be at par with the other people he was taking classes with; people who had done well in school? In his search for answers he found himself migrating toward education classes where he was drawn to books on mind/brain science and how we process data and create understanding. This in turn led him to classes and books about alternate ways of learning and teaching. He was to discover that people learn in different ways and it had little to do with IQ. Some people learned better visually and some people were auditory learners, while a third group did better by being immersed in the situation in a hands-on manner. Here he found some answers, but it wasn't until he met Henry that the pieces really started falling into place.

The Superintendent

The first time I saw Henry in action was in a town council meeting in a small town within Henry's school district. The town had been struggling with the issue of a proposed new park. Should they spend their limited funds to build a park along the creek on a sizable tract of land that had been donated to the town? It had been a contentious issue for months, and the anger and frustration of the residents was coming to a head. At this meeting the warring factions were at loggerheads, the meeting was deteriorating and seemed within minutes of erupting into shouting and name calling.

It was a small town surrounded by farms and orchards and the people in attendance were of the Oregon vernacular, fiercely independent small-town farmers, orchardists and shopkeepers. Henry, as was usual in the evening, had left his necktie behind and was dressed much as the farmers and orchardists did, in shirt sleeves and work pants. He sat quietly and listened to the people struggle with the issue throughout the meeting. Frustrations had about reached boiling point and the mayor seemed ready to adjourn the meeting to avoid trouble, again without being able to call for a vote to resolve the matter one way or the other.

It was at this time that Henry unwound his lanky frame and slowly stood up, like an old farmer stiff from a day of plowing getting ready to address the farm bureau. He began by saying he was sorry to intrude on their meeting and take up their time, but he was unclear on one or two points and hoped someone could explain them to him. The next half hour was pure small town magic. It seemed that nearly everyone on both sides of the issue was eager to explain to their school superintendent what he failed to grasp.

As soon as one question was worn out, Henry would ask another. Again and again, all of them were eager to help him understand. This went on for a time and, as it did, the rancor seemed to bleed out of the crowd and accord was growing as they proudly helped their superintendent figure it all out.

After Henry was finally satisfied and had all his questions answered, the tension was gone from the room and someone called for a vote on the issue. It passed easily and now years later the town is proud of a park with a bike and jogging path along the creek, that stretches for miles and serves the children and adults of the town well.

After the meeting, both sides seemed proud of their decision to move ahead and most of them came over to make sure that Henry fully understood what had just happened. He listened graciously to each person, thanking them for helping him get a handle on the issues and then congratulating them all for their decision to move ahead on the park. I think I know what Henry's response would be if you were to ask him about that meeting now. He would probably pause for a minute and say, "Well, I guess I don't remember that one."

The wily ol' superintendent started both the teacher and his odd mix of kids on a new course of their lives one winter day in December and later, when asked, wouldn't even remember doing so. Maybe he was just doing his job solving problems and, in this case, changing the world for a teacher, a little girl and a ragtag bunch of misfits as well as inspiring a bunch of bright kids on to better things. He seemingly did this without even remembering he had done anything special.

Maybe that's the way it's supposed to be; a conscious, aware person going about his normal day, doing the normal things required of them, unaware that they are sometimes doing something that may be life-changing for another person. Most of us forget about the ordinary that we do every day and only remember the "important" things. That day Henry was just doing what superintendents do, solve problems. So his actions didn't seem to qualify as anything important enough to remember, particularly years later.

Later in the year, Henry would say he, "discovered" an innovative teacher and an odd assortment of kids, and out of curiosity, got involved in the program. For whatever reason, the teacher was experimenting with an eclectic and unusual collection of methods to connect with the bored and hard-to-reach kids of the school and Henry began adding his ideas to the mix and soon jumped in with both feet.

Chapter 6

An Unreachable Girl Shows Up

"Unreachable" children come in two varieties, those with broken, and unbroken, spirits. The hardest to reach are the quiet, apathetic ones. Give me the angry rebellious ones anytime, their spirits are intact, the gold just waiting to be found.

She was brought into my classroom by the principal and two deputy sheriffs; a little waif of a child, probably not five feet tall and less than 75 pounds soaking wet. Why it took two of them, I didn't know, but would find out soon enough.

I already had more problem children in my classroom than I really knew what to do with, but there seemed to be a never-ending supply of such kids at this school, each with more problems than the last. But when Wesley explained to me that this was her last chance, that if I couldn't make room for her she was going straight to MacLaren, what could I say? MacLaren was not a good place for such a little girl.

MacLaren was part of Oregon's correctional system, a long-term housing facility for incorrigible juvenile girls the system had given up on. As Oregon's final answer to female juvenile delinquents, I knew that in reality MacLaren was just a finishing school for girls on their way to a life of welfare, drugs and crime, and she would probably remain there until she was 18. So I said of course there was room for her. After all, what was one more little kid?

From the very first, Teresa was a real conundrum, a child obviously in deep pain, a child who for the first three months in my classroom didn't even acknowledge my presence. She ignored me as surely as if I weren't in the room. Her contempt for me was as palpable as her disdain for being forced to be there at all. I marveled at her ability to avoid all eye contact. No matter how or when I happened to look her way, even when I just scanned my eyes across the classroom, she would always just happen to be suddenly looking elsewhere. It was uncanny. It was like she had a sixth sense, a built-in radar or avoidance system. I knew she was really just watching and waiting, but for what?

Teresa had a sixth sense about something else too—boys. She soon had a small circle of admirers at her beck and call. At first I hoped this would prove to be an avenue into Teresa's world through some of the boys I had established rapport with, but as time went on it became apparent that this wasn't going to happen. I suppose that was when I began to wonder what in the world had happened to Teresa and whether I could even help her. What did I really know about helping broken kids anyway? I was a just a renegade adult still struggling to overcome my own battered experiences in a school room.

Arguably, Teresa was the most "broken" kid I was ever to meet. She was withdrawn, sullen and non-communicative for the first few months she was in my classroom. She was the child who really tested my ideas and desire to work with problem kids, and she would continue to haunt me for more than twenty years after I left education. It was my experience with her and the other really hard cases that caused me to read and study about learning problems long after leaving education. She is the reason I am writing this book now.

At the time, it remained an open question whether I had the ability or skills needed to deal with such profound problems. It was Teresa who brought up deep feelings of inadequacy and shame in me which were the residue of my own failings as a child.

Was this fear that I would fail Teresa after I had glibly assumed that I could make a difference in her life? Right now, I couldn't even reach her, let alone have an actual conversation. I confess to thinking at times that perhaps Teresa would have been better off in the MacLaren Youth Correctional Facility. Maybe someone there could reach her.

The one thing about Teresa that was encouraging was her will to fight. Because she was a scrapper and a fighter, it didn't seem like that fire was about to go out anytime soon. It seemed that with such dogged determination and stubborn will, if she ever could be reached, maybe, just maybe, I might be able to help. But then for God's sake, what did I know about what she needed?

Chapter 7

A Key Technique

William Glasser's book, **Schools Without Failure**, *was the most revolutionary book on education published to date. His Glasser Class Meeting was one of the reasons we had the results we did.*

The purpose of a Glasser Class Meeting was to open up dialogue amongst the members of the class, challenge their beliefs, and stimulate critical thinking. The role of the teacher was only that of moderator. He was not even to have an opinion or make a judgment on any topic that was brought up by the kids in the meeting. In addition, whatever was talked about in the meeting was to stay within the room.

It took a few weeks for the class to realize that this was their meeting. At first they dealt with the inane, as children will do when they think their opinions don't count anyway. However, when they found that no topic was out of bounds and they weren't being judged on the validity of what they believed or thought, things changed. When they found they were free to ask questions and make observations they had never asked adults before, the barriers dropped away and the class migrated to surprisingly complex and interesting issues.

For example, one of the less controversial questions that came up, but demonstrated their viewpoint versus mine, was a question Randy McCarty asked me during one of the meetings. He said curiously, "Mr. Smith, how does it feel to be so old you know you're about to die?"

Being only 27 at the time, I was a bit amused for a moment. I guess to a twelve-year old, I seemed ancient. After thinking a bit, I replied, "Well, put it this way, Randy; when I'm 97, you'll be 82 and we'll sit together in our rocking chairs on the front porch of the old folks' home." The class stared at me, lost for a bit, and then they seemed to internalize this new information with grins.

Randy became a lifelong friend and when he was over fifty, I asked what he thought about that question now, since he was about twice as old as I was at the time. He laughed and said, "Mr. Smith, I have kids older than you were at the time."

Part of a Glasser Class Meeting.

A Key Technique

More of the same Glasser Class Meeting.

Chapter 8

The Crystal Radio Affair

It's hard to keep them down on the farm when they have seen gay Paree!

In the days before the digital age of technology, the magic of being able to make your own radio was pretty heady stuff in the minds of many young boys. When I was teaching at Phoenix Elementary School, I found that while the age of crystal radios was past, it still amazed the class to hear that kids could piece together a homemade radio with fifty cents worth of parts that would pull music and sound out of the air without the use of a battery. I'm not sure it has the same allure today, but I suspect it still would if presented in the right way. It was sheer magic to most of the class to think that they, with their own two hands, a bit of wire, a scrap of wood and parts, could make a radio that would actually tune into the BBC or Radio Moscow.

I suppose I told them at some point about how I used to lie awake at night under the covers of my bed in the dark, listening to Radio Moscow and the BBC with a radio that I had cobbled together myself. My mother thought I was asleep while this was going on, and she never quite understood how I could sleep for ten hours and wake up the next morning exhausted. Of course I was tired, I listened to radio stations in what were "exotic and fascinating places" to a farm kid from rural southern Oregon.

I told them how I had stretched an antenna from my upstairs bedroom window to the top of a tall cedar tree out by the barn, a good 200 feet away. And I told them how to salvage antenna wire from old automobile generators. When they heard this radio didn't have to be plugged into a socket, didn't need batteries, and how it just ran off the energy of the radio waves that filled the air, they were hooked. The fact that I was listening to radio stations on the other side of the world was almost beyond belief. Maybe that was what really excited them the most because this all was still before the era of satellites and international broadcasts.

The seeds for building their own radios had been planted in the minds of the class and the plan was made. They were shown how to scrounge wire from a used car generator and soon, after they had recruited their uncles or grandfathers, they started coming to school with coil after coil of wire. I went to a local manufacturer of small wood products and one of his products was a small pine board he provided to another manufacturer as the wooden base of an old-fashioned rat trap. He had plenty of rejects and was happy to donate them to our cause. The small, half-inch-thick pine boards, about four inches by six inches, were perfect bases on which to build our radios.

For a dollar or two we ordered a fistful of diodes, the critical ingredient for a crystal radio, and we were ready to embark on this new project. A few weeks later antennas sprouted from the windows of Smith's classroom to the tops of the nearby cedar trees surrounding the building and I didn't even want to know how they all got there.

It still amazes me how many grandfathers could still find the old headsets they used on their own crystal radios when they were little boys. This was a lucky break, because a crystal radio takes a special old-fashioned headset with extremely low power requirements. Modern headsets are made to work for radios with amplifiers, which require batteries.

Soon Mr. Smith's room was full of kids, each moving to a different beat of the music from their crystal radios which only they could hear. It seemed that I had added a new problem for my critics in the community to talk about. Now the kids in Mr. Smith's class just sat around all day chewing gum, making popcorn and listening to Radio Moscow with their crystal radios. That is, all except Teresa. She just sat there. Sure, it was early in the school year. I still had until June.

Soon the crystal radio fad faded. Most of the class was on to other things, but a few of the boys stuck to radios. I showed the interested ones how to add a transistor and a speaker, which required a battery. Our school library had located some old radio books in a back room

A few crystal radios.

of one of the county libraries with simple diagrams this group of kids really dug into. Soon some of the kids had radios with three or four transistors and a volume control for the speakers. These kids were in hog heaven and way ahead of my knowledge of radio schematics. In fact, I no longer knew enough to help them much when they had a problem. Still, I should have realized it wouldn't stop there. Somewhere in that class an idea was percolating about the radios that would again amaze me as to the group's resourcefulness.

Chapter 9

Bobby James Smith

The teachers' break room can easily be the road to perdition for many a kid. Once they get a reputation, it's pretty hard to shake.

Working with kids others have given up on has it rewards. It's a little like treasure hunting. You never know where it will be found; and sometimes in your digging you can find an old lump that doesn't look like much at all, but when you scratch the surface you find pure gold.

My first encounter with Bobby James Smith was on the playground. He wasn't in my class, but I was assured by the first grade teachers that I could definitely have him. As I kept hearing more of this supposed holy terror in the teachers' break room I kept wishing he were in my class.

Now, the teachers' break room is where more kids get put on the road to perdition by their teachers than in any other place. Teachers, many times overworked and underpaid, enter the break room relating their latest scrap with a student. If another teacher or two has had a bad experience with this child, it's easy to begin to decide there's a problem here. In the process, the die is cast. The kid gets a label of problem child, or troubled child, and seems to do his dead-level best to live up to it. By the time the child reaches the next grade level, his reputation has preceded him.

These tidbits of "my student is worse than your student" can sometimes doom children like Bobby to grade school hell from the very first day of school. For that reason, I always refused to read the cumulative record that comes with each kid. I didn't want to be disavowed of the notion that each kid was special and had hidden talents, and I usually found out that they did.

Each morning brought a new tale of misbehavior about Bobby's meanness and rebellion. From the stories, I began to develop a mental image of the larger-than-life, man-sized boy who was undoubtedly a menace to the teacher and whose lashing-out was a threat to the safety of the children and the school itself. Somehow, I doubted it.

In the celebrity world, the highest ranking possible is when someone becomes known by one name only, such as Cher or Jackie. It was a little different at our school. Here one knew for sure that a student was thought to be on the road to federal prison when the teachers would call them by all their given names such as, in this case, Bobby James Smith.

The day I was to finally meet this menace was on a Monday morning early in the second week of summer school. The whereabouts of Bobby James Smith had been discovered, and the posse was forming. I'm not sure what caused the ruckus but when it blew up, apparently the other teachers swarmed to the call for help. As the only male teacher on staff at that time, of course I was called. Because of the mental image I had of him, I ran there at top speed.

My first encounter with Bobby James Smith was something to behold. He was about the sorriest bogeyman I could imagine. He was about four feet tall and only weighed about 60 pounds, but was he a scrapper! He was fighting, and successfully holding off, three older boys, all twice his size. He fought like a whirling dervish as his fists flailed every which-way. Finally, I managed to wade in and grab him by the collar and the seat of his pants, literally picking him up, and carrying him out of there, all the while dodging his fists and feet as they continued to flail the air.

As the situation was brought under control, I noticed he was pasty white and shaking like a leaf, which I assumed was from the struggle. But later, something just didn't ring true and I began to hang around his classroom in my spare minutes.

He certainly was a handful and seemed to have a hair trigger. Many times he would get off the bus in the mornings having already been in a fight with a bigger kid or the bus driver. It seemed he was a severely troubled kid and expecting him to get much out of his studies when he was in a constant state of agitation and rage doomed him to failure.

Bobby, as well as several other boys, were the topic of constant concerned discussion that spring. I finally decided that something had to be done. I volunteered to take a group of the worst male offenders on a camping trip and see whether I could bond with them, or at least learn something helpful. So some reassigning of students was done, and I began to plan a weekend camping trip with five of the biggest troublemakers as my new charges.

We were given a small budget, and as a group we went into great detail planning what we would take along for food. On the morning of departure, we all went shopping. These kids bought enough food to feed a small army and that was when I realized I would be busy with just the cooking alone.

The first evening I managed to come up with some soup, milk and sandwiches. But it was the next morning I dreaded because they had decided they wanted pancakes, sausages and omelets. I wasn't too sure how I was going to pull that off with one skillet, but we'd just have to make do. I found out long ago that hungry boys weren't too picky when it came to food. I planned to work them hard and keep them hungry.

The next morning I was awakened by the smell of sausage and eggs cooking when dawn wasn't yet in full swing. At first I was disoriented, as no one else had been in the campground the night before. When I finally got my bearings, Bobby had already made breakfast for all of us, and had done a far better job than I could have. There was a great stack of pancakes and bacon, and the eggs were done sunny side up. He seemed to be in his element. When the other kids got up, he was seven feet tall in their eyes and in mine as well.

He did all the cooking for the rest of the weekend. He owned the kitchen and loved doing it. Here was a troubled kid taking control of the situation, not only in cooking but also in most everything else we did that weekend. He was a natural leader, and the other boys realized it and followed his lead even though he was the youngest in the pack. It was obvious he was used to foraging for himself, and apparently had received at least a little parenting from his father or mother somewhere along the way.

On that weekend I found that when Bobby was well fed, he was a boy anybody could be proud of and enjoy being around. I came back after that weekend wondering how many other kids with behavior problems, in a program for troubled kids, simply had a blood sugar problem or were just plain hungry.

So the next Monday I brought a gallon of milk and a box of cereal from home, and just happened to be going by when he got off his bus. Again, he had that set to his jaw which said "stay out of my way," but as of yet he hadn't launched himself into anyone. In my most friendly jolly good teacher mode, I said, "Hi, Bobby James Smith, how are you doing?" He eyed me suspiciously but said, "Hi, Mr. Smith" and fell into step beside me.

Then, seeing the milk, he said, "Whatcha got the milk for?" "Well, Bobby, I didn't have time for breakfast, want to join me?" "Sure" was the too-quick reply, and I knew I had him pegged. So we opened up the cafeteria, found a couple of bowls and had some cereal, and I just happened to find a boiled egg in my pocket. By that time he was in great spirits and the mood lasted all day.

So that became a morning ritual, the two of us having breakfast together in the cafeteria before school. The change in him was just short of miraculous. He went all that week without a single incident.

At the staff meeting on Friday, I told the principal what I learned. I found out that Bobby lived alone with his dad, who didn't wake up early and Bobby had to get himself up and ready for school. Sometimes there wasn't a thing in the house to eat or, at best, candy. He was coming to school probably with no breakfast and sometimes with nothing but a candy bar the night before.

It seemed obvious to me that he had some sort of blood sugar issue and that triggered his rages. For anyone who knew what that was like, as I did, it was easy to understand his outbursts. A box of granola, a quart of milk and some cheese soothed the beast in him, and by summer's end the stories of Bobby James Smith were slowly but surely forgotten.

Whatever happened to Bobby, I don't know. But I found in him just what I had found in most of the "hard cases." Somewhere in almost all kids was something worth believing in, and while it took longer in some than in others, it was always worth waiting for. Give me the fighters and the rebels every time. These kids still have their spirit intact. It is the sullen, apathetic ones you really have to worry about. However, if we can just plant a seed of hope in a fighter and then love them, they'll usually be fine, especially if we catch them young enough. Once the spirit is broken, it is a long road back, but even then there is still hope, as I was to find out.

Chapter 10

The Crystal Radio Goes Entrepreneurial

Involving kids in a small, age-appropriate entrepreneurial enterprise is a valid way to teach a variety of skills and subjects to an assortment of interests and abilities, all at the same time and with each child learning at his own pace and level of ability.

It wasn't long until nearly every kid in the school wanted a crystal radio just for the novelty of it. Some of the little rascals in the class were even making money on the side by charging kids from other classes to listen to their radio. Then one day one of the boys in our Glasser Class Meeting asked why we couldn't build crystal radios for sale. So a few were wired together, but someone in the class soon figured out, with true business sense, how to make the task easier. It would be easier to sell the parts with an instruction manual than to sell assembled radios. And so it was that Mr. Smith's class got into the radio kit business.

It soon sank in that such an enterprise would take working capital. Having a rule in my class that we didn't ask mom and dad to finance our field trips or other things they wanted to do as a class, they had to earn the money. So the head scratching began. The kids wanted to know where other businesses got financing for their ideas. I told them of the various ways, and added that many borrowed it from the bank.

So the next question was obvious. Would the bank lend us money for our business venture? Good question.

It was a small town with only one bank and, fortunately, the banker was a friendly sort. Without their knowledge I visited the banker ahead of time and explained what the class had in mind. He was fascinated and said he was sure he would enjoy doing it for us. He agreed to lend the money only if they had done their homework on the product being sold. They could expect some hard questions from him. I relayed this to the class, and when suddenly faced with reality they began to wonder whether the $50 they thought they needed to finance their enterprise was enough, or perhaps too much, especially when it dawned on them they would really have to pay it back.

The class decided they'd better go over the business plan they put together and make sure they understood any questions that might be asked. We did some role playing, with me pretending to be the banker. They looked again at the radio parts catalog that someone had procured to figure the cost of parts and shipping. That was when it was discovered they hadn't even thought about how many radio kits they wanted to make. After much discussion, thirty kits were decided upon. They really wanted to make more, but the reality of borrowing more money and having more to pay back kept them in check.

A great deal of time went into finding out how we could collect the parts for the 30 kits and the costs involved. The new telephone was busy all the time. Meetings were held and plans made, and old ideas scrapped as new ones evolved.

I smiled to myself as I looked around the room. Honest learning was taking place in five or six different little groups, all doing different things. They had broken themselves up into small groups according to their interests and natural skills . They were solving real problems. For me it didn't get any better than this; and it worked so well because it was their idea, their plan and they were responsible for it and for paying back the loan. I was just along for the ride, and to sometimes give advice if they came to me with a question.

The aspect of this sort of education that has always amazed me is the level at which a classroom operates collectively, if the energy and intellect of the kids can be harnessed and all pointed in the same general direction. In these situations, it seemed that all ideas that could possibly occur to me could also strike any of the thirty kids, but collectively many more. It was similar to the idea that a handful of kids were a real match in a chess game for Henry, who was very good on the chessboard. Individually, none of them would have a chance against him, but collectively they were a worthy opponent to any challenger.

The best typewriter a dollar will buy.

Soon the class informed me they were ready to face the banker. They added that since they were fully aware that it wasn't my style to do the talking for them, they had made sure their president, vice president, secretary and treasurer were ready to do so. The class knew this was their idea and they were on their own. Sure, I would accompany them, but this was their gig.

The president and the class officers did a whiz-bang job of presenting their case as the rest of the class crowded into the banker's office and watched. The questions that the class officers couldn't answer always seemed to be the area of expertise of someone else in the class who they would turn to for help. Less than an hour later, after the class officers had signed the note, they opened a checking account in the name of the class, and I wasn't even permitted to be a signer on that either. These kids were taking full responsibility, as it was intended.

A rudimentary set of records for bookkeeping was set up, and the treasurer became an actual treasurer with a checkbook and money in the bank. Now the real work began. It was an exciting morning when the group responsible for ordering the parts actually put the order together and calculated the shipping charges. The treasurer wrote the check and a few kids carried the envelope to the post office.

All this time, another group was working on the instruction booklet, which turned out to be a larger task than they had envisioned. As they settled down to their task, instructions were written. Other students were handed the instructions to see whether they could assemble a radio with the parts, pretending they didn't know how to do it. At first there wasn't much correlation between what was written and what they had to do to build a radio. Then diagrams were added and the directions rewritten and rewritten again, until anyone in the class could read them and pretty much put the parts together into a working radio. This took several weeks, but I doubt those kids could have learned any more about logic and English than they did during that time. Finally, something resembling a small booklet of instructions was typed up on our old typewriter. Then duplicated on the mimeograph machine in the school office and added to the kit.

During this time, we also delved into the process of how we would assemble all the parts into a kit, using the assembly line idea. Flowcharts were drawn on the blackboard and another group wrote instructions for each station. Finally the day came when all the parts arrived and the class would begin to assemble their first batch of radio kits.

Tables were moved around the room to reflect the flowchart on the blackboard, parts distributed to the different stations, the stations manned and the class went into production at about 10:30 one morning. By lunchtime they had thirty radio kits neatly lined up on the windowsill in plastic sandwich bags, ready for our sales force to do their job. The class bank balance was notably depleted.

Radio Kit Assembly Line.

By the end of the second day, all the radio kits were sold and the bank account held almost $100. Boy, they were fired up. That was about the time their problems began. It seemed that most of their customers couldn't figure out how to assemble their radios using the instructions the booklet provided. Some refunds were made and some of the radio kits were assembled for the buyers. Then it was back to the drawing board with the instruction booklet. They found it was easy to write directions for something they already knew how to build, but it didn't work so well for customers with no background knowledge to begin with. The rewriting continued until someone from outside the class could actually put a kit together by reading the directions, without help from anyone in the class.

Fresh from their success, they were ready to plunge ahead. They were confident from the orders and it was time to gear up and assemble another batch. Before they received the parts for these kits, two other teachers in our building ordered radio kits for their classes! Then an order came in from a class outside of our school district. Either word was spreading by word of mouth or we had a really good sales force.

It was a good thing the end of the year was near, or I'm not sure I could have gotten them back to the regular classroom activities.

Renegade Teacher

Somewhere along the way they decided to repay their loan. Interest was calculated, and the banker was invited to visit. They proudly presented the check for the loan and the interest due along with a free radio kit, as pictures were taken by the class photographer with their new Polaroid camera purchased with radio money.

The students paid the banker back in full for the loan.

As the end of the year approached, another problem loomed large on their horizon and much time was devoted to finding its solution. It seems that after paying their loan, they still had more than $350 in their bank account. An end-of-the-year party had long been planned, but that would only set them back $25 or $30. Deciding what to do with the rest of the money was an interesting challenge for them. At first they talked about another really big party, until they found out how much cupcakes, punch and ice cream cost. It would be hard to spend that much money that way. There was talk of splitting the money amongst the class, but nobody seemed to have much enthusiasm for that. They had earned it as a class and wanted to do something with it as a class.

About this time, someone suggested creating some sort of a memorial for their favorite librarian, who had died during the year. She had been a real friend to our class and its programs. We used the library a great deal for looking up information on a wide variety of topics. The librarian borrowed book after book from the county library system on topics you wouldn't expect a fifth or sixth grader to be interested in. Now the class wanted to do something in her honor.

They decided to design, build and finish a bookshelf which would hold the library's collection of all the books that were Caldecott award winners, the librarian's favorite books for kids. Most of the class was proficient at putting a beautiful furniture finish on any kind of wood. In fact, many of the kids made their own chessboards and finished them with multiple coats of polyurethane hand-rubbed to perfection. Since the sanding and polishing of a piece of wood was something they could do in class while reading or working on other things, some of them had put twenty coats of finish on their chessboards. They sanded and hand-polished between each coat, resulting in a mirror-like finish they were proud of.

Unbeknownst to me, some of the boys on the "acquisition" committee climbed into the second floor attic of our ancient school building and cut a five foot piece of 4x12 rough-sawn timber from one of the braces that held up the roof. When they brought it into the class I didn't think much about it. These kids had already proved to be resourceful and I assumed one of them had brought it from home or from their grandfather's barn. Who knew with that bunch?

The shelf turned out to be beautiful. The plank from the attic was old enough to be from an era when all the logs were first cut into thick slabs as wide as the original log, with the bark left on both outer edges. The class left the bark intact and then sanded the rough-sawn surfaces smooth. They lovingly finished it with nearly 30 coats of hand-rubbed polyurethane, with everyone in the class taking turns, until it looked like it was embedded in a coat of glass. I imagine it is still in the library of that school just where the kids mounted it. But I doubt if the school knows the history of its origin and the love and endless hours a motley bunch of kids poured into this gift to their beloved librarian.

I wasn't to find out the source of the wood until after it was mounted in the library, and then it was too late to do anything about it. However, since the building didn't shake any worse than it had before and it was slated for demolition to make way for a new building anyway, I thought discretion the better part of valor. When I talked with the acquisition crew, they said, "Don't worry Mr. Smith, it really wasn't supporting much and besides, we left the other six feet there." At the time I decided just to sit on the information because creating a big stink by going public with this bit of information wouldn't put the timber back in the attic. Besides, I didn't want Wesley to have a heart attack after all we had put him through.

After buying polyurethane and sandpaper for the bookshelf, they still faced the dilemma of what to do with the rest of the money. Surprisingly, they became very interested in local charities and a great deal of time and effort went into studying which charity they would like to support. In the end they split the several hundred dollars among two or three different charities.

Someone's radio bites the dust.

Chapter 11

Crack Shows—or Does It?

*Like most new beginnings, it's not all smooth sailing.
Sometimes it's hard to tell if there is any movement at all,
or whether it's just smoke and no fire.*

As the weeks went on, I was amazed at Teresa's ability to sit in that classroom and never touch a book, never pick up a pencil, never open a notebook or pick up a piece of paper. What was she doing inside that little mind of hers? Other than a wary whispered comment to a boy now and then, she just sat there. So we settled in for the long haul. I knew that I couldn't do anything for Teresa until she would engage, if then. Coercion wouldn't work on this child, if indeed it ever worked on any child for very long. It would take patience and time. Patience and time I had plenty of, but with this one I wondered if that was enough. Little did I imagine what I was in for. It's probably well that I didn't, or I might just have thrown in the towel.

I continued to wonder what could have happened at this young age to make her so cynical, so distrusting of teachers, or was it just men? Again I thought I knew the answer.

As fall faded into winter, Teresa never strayed very far from my mind and, as I lay awake at night, doubts crowded in. What was I doing?

Renegade Teacher

What did I know about fixing troubled children when parts of me were still just a broken little boy myself?

All the old trusty platitudes about believing in children seemed empty and hollow. What good were platitudes if she wouldn't talk to me or even look my way when I addressed her by name? I was shut out of her life. The old reassurances that I would give myself, that the child will rise to meet your expectations, sounded delusional and dead.

As Christmas approached, I began to face the very real possibility that I wouldn't be able to reach Teresa. I began to wonder whether I should find a place for her with someone who knew what she needed, someone who might be able to help her where I couldn't. Then when I least expected it, the first crack in her exterior appeared.

One of the things I found effective in working with all children was engaging them in some sort of journaling or creative writing. We didn't have too many things that were mandatory in my classroom, but quiet reading time and journaling time was sacred. Whether or not they wanted to read or journal, they were required to sit quietly so others could. Teresa only sat and stared.

This particular morning I was using my old tried-and-true ploy of starting a story and letting the child write the ending. My ploy was simple. It was my job to create and tell a story in a fashion that would involve them and when I got to the most exciting spot, where the animal or hero was in great peril, I would stop and let them write their own ending. The next day I would read the best of their stories to the class. Of course, I would add all the theatrics I could muster to make even the duller stories teem with excitement. Most of the kids loved it and eagerly participated, just for the fun of it and hoping for the honor of having their stories read to the class.

This particular day I was telling a story about a scared mother rabbit out in a snowstorm, struggling to find food for her starving babies back in the den. Across a deep layer of snow and in bitter cold, she was running to avoid becoming dinner for the hungry wolf. But the wolf was faster than the mother rabbit and was gaining on her. Closer and closer the wolf came until the rabbit was able to hear his breathing over her own panting. Just as his jaws closed around her neck, I stopped the story and left the students to finish it.

This time, to my amazement, Teresa picked up a pencil, grabbed a piece of paper and started scribbling furiously. She wrote with an anger and vengeance that I had never seen in a child simply writing a story. Her face was contorted in rage and I thought she would break her pencil.

When she was done, she charged up to my desk, and without looking at me slammed the paper down and stomped back to her seat. I tried to act uninterested as I stuffed stories into my briefcase to read later.

That night as I read over their stories, I was struck with the fury Teresa had managed to cram into a few simple, misspelled sentences on a crumpled piece of paper. I had never seen such violence, anger and frustration expressed from such simple sentences.

Now the other part of my job as the teacher was to iron out the paper, decipher the writing, and be able to read it to the class the next day. It can be challenging to find their voice on a crumpled scrap of paper, maybe erased and rewritten until there were holes in the paper. But, to let the child hear their voice and to realize he or she has something to contribute can be magic.

The next day when I read Teresa's story to the class, the raw power of her words stunned the rest of the class and when I finished, they all just sat there in silence, not knowing what to say.

When I read the stories back to the class I never revealed names. That was part of the game and it allowed the writer to be anonymous, or not, at their choosing. But when I read Teresa's story, she was so vulnerable that even without a name she felt like everyone knew instantly that this was hers. When they sat there in stunned silence, Teresa read this as rejection and a personal rebuke. She rose up out of her seat as though she'd been attacked. She came up to my desk in a rage and grabbed the sheet of paper out of my hand and slammed it into the trash can. Then in a sullen fury she once again stomped back to her seat. Hmm, I wondered how long it would be until she ventured out of her shell again.

Chapter 12

The Mouse Farm Enterprise

One secret of motivating a group of kids is to discover their perceived needs and to turn the responsibility for generating the money to meet those needs over to them. In fact, few things motivate kids more than the prospect of making money for the things they really want, particularly when the activity is free from adult intervention and value judgment.

It is essential and fundamental to this method of teaching that children see themselves as responsible for generating money for any monetary needs the class might have. Dragging the money out of their parents or grandparents defeats the purpose of this type of learning activity. After the class decided they really did have a need for extra money, everyone went on a mission of seek and discovery, looking for valid money-making ideas which would adapt to our classroom and its talents.

Once an endeavor was decided upon, the real work began. Here, all the reading, writing, math, group cooperation and bookkeeping, plus a dozen other topics, just naturally became part of solving the problems along the way.

This particular year, a boy brought in a magazine article which said scientific laboratories paid over $200 for a pair of white mice for laboratory work. His plan was to raise white mice for sale to laboratories. The idea was an immediate hit. There wasn't a kid in the room who didn't think they could raise white mice, and they could visualize their success already. So we had all the necessary components of a great learning experience. They had a plan. It was their idea and they felt confident they had the skills. The die was cast. They were to become mouse farmers. Little did they know what perils lay ahead. This group was to learn more about a wider variety of topics than they could have learned any other way.

One of my philosophies for working with children was to allow them to make honest mistakes and live with the consequences. While it seemed to me highly unlikely that a laboratory would shell out hard-earned money for a white mouse raised by a sixth grade class, many a business is started on a shakier premise than this one. They all had stars in their eyes, and that is the catalyst for learning and for overcoming insurmountable odds. The question now was, what would they learn?

When the class finished formulating their business plan, off we went to the bank to make the proposal and defend the idea. By this time the banker looked forward to hearing what the current class idea for making money was to be, and he greeted them with much enthusiasm. The proposal was made, and the banker listened while he asked them plenty of penetrating questions which caused much squirming. After due consideration, the loan was agreed to once again, papers were drawn up and the class officers bravely signed their names.

A checking account was opened in their name and as usual, the class officers were again the only signers on the account. I have always believed that one of the greatest components for eventual success was failure in age-appropriate doses. Learning from our failures can be a huge component of eventual success. If I hadn't failed at being a car salesman, I might still be selling cars and I was a lousy car salesman. So I tried as much as possible to allow the kids to make their own decisions and live with the results.

One kid donated a pair of white mice which I am sure the parents were glad to see go. Materials were purchased and a cage was built. Food was scrounged from the cafeteria, as well as brought from home, as our classroom became the breeding grounds for white mice. Soon our pair became six, as mice are wont to do, and 16 became 48 in an amazingly short time. We were in business.

Soon a faint odor began to emanate from Mr. Smith's classroom on the first floor of an old-fashioned, two-story brick elementary school building. I sensed trouble ahead but, true to my philosophy, I ignored it. If there were problems ahead, they were the class' problems, not mine; otherwise I was the only one who would do any learning.

Now it seemed that these smells began to waft up the stairwell. Of course, my popularity in the teachers' break room sank inversely with

The kids made Mouse Houses.

the odor levels on the upper floor, and soon the teachers were complaining to Wesley, and he was complaining to me. So in my inevitable fashion, I had Wesley attend one of the class' Glasser Class Meetings to voice the complaints directly to the class. At first the kids tended to downplay the issue, as they had grown accustomed to the odor.

However, it wasn't until the principal told the class that the mice had to go that they really got the message that they had a problem.

Accounting for the mouse business.

Now, nothing motivates a kid more than the threatened loss of a pet, and these kids had about sixty beloved pets at this time. The mice were usually out of their cages during most of the day, being held by various children as they went about their normal day in the classroom. By now the mice were part of the class, so you can imagine the level of anxiety this turn of events caused.

In addition to the loss of their pets, these young entrepreneurs were aghast at the prospect of losing their breeding stock and therefore losing the source of repayment of their loan. As the crisis built, I just sat back and watched. Committees were formed, meetings were held and solutions were proposed. The atmosphere was not only ripe with the odor, but ripe with opportunity for this class to do a lot of learning, if I didn't yield to the temptation to solve the problem myself.

After much angst and several meetings with the principal, the class finally talked him into allowing them to move their mice into an abandoned furnace room in the old gymnasium, away from the main school building. Another crisis averted.

Moving day saw over 100 white mice settled into their new quarters in new cages, built by some of the class from supplies purchased from their dwindling funds. Soon, all was calm in mousedom, but I suspected the calm would be short-lived as the number of residents was sure to increase dramatically with 100 breeding mice.

When the population of the mouse house exceeded 300, new complaints began to arise from the teachers who held PE classes in the rest of the gymnasium. Again, the complaints escalated quickly, growing into a crescendo, and again Wesley appeared at their Glasser Class Meeting with an order from "on high." They had three days to clean up the stench in the gym or the mice had to go, permanently this time. Apparently, the other teachers were refusing to go into the gym due to the odors emanating from the mouse house.

Once again meetings were held, running right on through recess and the noon hour, and solutions discussed.

I purposely still didn't go over to the mouse house. It was their idea and their problem, and the less I knew about it the easier it was to not offer solutions disguised as advice. Finally a committee came to me and pleaded for my help, and I agreed to become a consultant on the problem.

A meeting was called to work on the problem. Were the cages being cleaned regularly? Yes, originally daily and now twice a day. Was someone assigned to see that it was done properly and that the cages were being sanitized? Yes. Could I see the written check lists? OK. It all looked good, so after a meeting of all concerned I was no closer to any explanation than they were, so I finally agreed we all would visit the mouse house together.

Now it was the teacher's turn to do some learning. And I probably learned more about the teacher/learner equation that day than the five years studying childhood development in college and my three years of classroom experience combined. As the door to the mouse house opened and I stepped up into the room I spotted the problem instantly, as probably any adult would. I was dumbfounded, but apparently I had some life experience they hadn't encountered and it was hard to keep my mouth shut and let them encounter theirs.

Sometimes I felt I understood the workings of the kids' minds and sometimes I didn't. Now if I could just turn this into a teachable moment, we all would have learned something.

Indeed the cages were immaculate. That surely wasn't the problem, but the stench of mouse manure was definitely overpowering. I remember wondering if even the mice thought it stank in their house. Then, I asked who was on cleaning duty today and would they demonstrate cleaning a cage. Two of the kids leaped to their tasks. Great care was taken as the mice were removed from the cage and given to someone to hold. The thick layer of sawdust was carefully removed and placed on the floor in front of the cage. The cage was disinfected and the water bowl and feeding tin were cleaned. The student on cleaning duty proudly returned the mice to their cage and turned to me as I waited for them to continue. I still couldn't believe that no one else had spotted anything unusual.

Now, one editor who worked on the manuscript seemed to think this class must have been of less than average intelligence. I can assure you this group's IQ was above average. This was something else. And, I believe it is one of the reasons we fail to reach some kids sometimes.

Standing in front of me were most of the class members, and they had watched this demonstration with rapt attention as they stood atop the foot of sawdust already on the floor. They looked expectantly at me for my observations. Now the hard part for a teacher who is honestly interested in teaching instead of just telling—is keeping your mouth shut at a teachable moment.

Not one of the kids noticed there was anything strange in what they had observed, so I began to review what I had seen with a deeply puzzled look on my face, as though I were Sherlock Holmes considering a very difficult clue. "Let's see. You removed the mice from their cage and placed them where? Yes, right. Then you collected the sawdust from the cage, right? And you put it where?" As I waited for the cage cleaner to answer, you could have heard a pin drop as the rest of the class, along with their teacher, puzzled over this baffling problem. Then slowly it began to dawn on one girl as I watched an "aha!" moment move across her face. It was as if day was dawning.

She looked at me with a knowing grin on her face as she glanced down at the pile of sawdust on which we were standing. I smiled at her and winked, and together we just stood there.

Teaching logical thinking instead of subject matter turns regular teaching upside down. When I went into the mouse house and had to step up on a pile of sawdust left there after cleaning the cages, it was difficult not to say, "Hey, you dummies, clean up the sawdust on the floor and you won't have an odor problem." I think most teachers were trained to react that way; I know it was my inclination. In fact the teachers I had when I was in school thrilled at being the givers of knowledge, and spent all their time reacting that way. Maybe it was because of my time on a farm that I equated sawdust with manure; it was so obvious to me. However, these were kids from town and to them it was just a sawdust-covered floor. Now I had to just stand there, as that "aha!" moment spread across all their faces, and this incident became part of their own life experience, one they would not forget soon.

The fact that thirty children had walked in and out of that room and stood on that pile for weeks without connecting the odor problem with the sawdust simply meant this was something they had not yet experienced in their short lives. Of course we would not expect three-year-olds to see the connection, and I'm not sure at what grade I would expect it, but the fact no one in that particular class saw it was surprising.

I guess this is a good example of "there are no stupid questions," just questions to which we don't have the answers. However, if I thought this had been a great crisis which provided valuable learning, it was nothing compared to what was on the horizon. The learning for this bunch of mouse farmers was really just beginning.

Chapter 13

Billy Johnson and his Whiskey Bottles

I knew from the beginning this boy would do fine in life. It's surprising what you can learn by watching kids play marbles for "keeps." And, life is for "keeps."

One thing I couldn't help thinking about as I worked with these challenging kids was, what would become of them in a few years? One little boy eased my mind about his future one spring. He showed up one morning holding a small antique wooden box with "Bonded Whiskey" still faintly visible on the side. It had wooden dividers which formed 12 places for antique, pintsize pumpkinseed whiskey flasks, six complete with bottles and six empty spaces.

"Billy, wow, that's pretty neat. Where did you get that," I asked? He explained how he had been with his granddad under his granddad's house and how he had seen the box sitting on top of a large timber. His granddad said he could have it and so he brought it to school.

"What are you going to do with it, Billy?" I asked. He replied that he was going to sell the bottles. Since I like antique bottles and these were as nice a little pumpkinseed flask as I had ever seen, I asked Billy what he wanted for one. He said six dollars, so I bought one. Later that day I saw another teacher with one. Then the janitor showed up with

Renegade Teacher

one, as did the principal. Pretty soon I had counted eight and smelled a rat. The next morning as Billy entered the classroom, his box had five more flasks in it, and I beckoned him over to the desk.

"W'w-what did I d'do, Mr. Smith?" he stammered sheepishly as he approached the desk. "Aha!", now it was "Mr. Smith" instead of just "Smith," I thought to myself. "Am I in trouble?" he asked. "I don't know, Billy, but last weekend you told me you found six whiskey bottles under your granddad's house, and you have sold eight that I know of and you still have five in your box. Can you explain that?"

"Mr. Smith, I'll...I'll give their money back!" he stammered. "No, no, not so fast, Billy; first just tell me what's going on." So in great fear, Billy told me his story. It seems he had sold all 6 of his bottles the first day for $6.00 each. On the way home with a pocket full of money, he happened to see some of the same bottles in an antique store window for just $3.50 each. At that point Billy had his own "aha!" moment, and filled his box all over again.

"Do I have to give them their money back, Mr. Smith?" he asked. "No, Billy, you keep it. You didn't do particularly wrong and you'll do just fine in this world." And he did. Last I knew, little Billy owned a couple of convenience stores and several pieces of rental property. He had a lovely wife and together they had raised six wonderful daughters who were growing up to become part of the solution to the world's problems, not part of the problem. In my book, that's a clear success, so Billy gets an A in my book.

Chapter 14

The Grim Reaper Visits Mousedom

Nothing like a good crisis to stimulate learning, but only the one who owns the crisis does any learning.

As the weeks rolled along and the mouse population grew, I sat back wondering what new calamity would befall my budding entrepreneurs next, as there was sure to be one. What new learning experience lay just around the corner? I didn't have to wait long to find out.

It started when two girls, with tears streaming down their faces, came running into the classroom and up to my desk. One of them had in her cupped hands the body of Cleo, her pet mouse. (I still haven't figured out how the kids could tell one white mouse from another and, of course, the kids thought I was slow because they could and I couldn't.) She relayed how she had gone to get her particular pet and found him in his present state lying in the cage. Soon another kid brought in the second dead mouse. The next day there were seven and the following day twice that.

If you would like a way to get a kid's attention, let them become emotionally involved with animals that start dying. I guarantee you will have one engaged class of kids who, with a little guidance, will be very ready to go into a problem-solving mode and work on solving it day and night. Now another great learning experience was developing, if I was just clever enough to simply stay out of the way and let the learning happen.

I wasn't too concerned because just by looking I had a pretty good idea what the problem was. If I was right in my quick analysis of the situation, it wasn't transmittable; it was dietary. I hadn't seen too many cases of scurvy, but when I saw these mice it rang a bell from pictures I had seen of animals with scurvy. The dead mice were hunched back and skinny. Also their feet and toes were drawn up in the peculiar manner indicative of that disease. I decided to mosey over to see if I could confirm what I thought. When I arrived I indeed noted that most of the surviving mice were already walking around on the tips of their toes with their backs all hunched up. The mounting death toll would continue.

Since this was not a threat from a pathogen, I would wait to see what developed. I knew it would be interesting and, again, probably also a great learning motivator for the class. If I handled this correctly, the kids would learn more about health and diet in the coming days than they would learn in eight years of grade school health classes, and that is what school is all about, right?

The level of concern of the class soon reached a fevered pitch. Even the library staff was put into crisis mode as they ordered every book they could find in the County's main catalog having anything to do with health or disease in animals. Books and magazines were devoured. The telephone was a godsend and in constant use, as any health official who had the bad fortune of having their name listed in the public record was contacted. We had rigged up a small speaker so we could all listen to what was being said; and the classroom became Crisis Central. The list of people they could think of to call was endless. If they were listed in the phone book and had any relation to animals or disease, they were targeted and called.

Each day the pressure to solve this problem mounted, right along with the death toll. It reached its apex when more mice were dying than were being born, at a net loss. This threatened the business enterprise and tugged at their hearts. To say they burned the midnight oil was an understatement.

At the end of the first week, with the death rate now in the 35-a-day range, the first eureka moment occurred. Dirk came in from the library and came directly to my desk and quietly said, "I think I know why the mice are dying, Mr. Smith; I think they have scurvy." He went on to lay out his case, based on a book telling of sailors getting scurvy from the lack of fruits and vegetables on long ocean voyages. He further explained how the ship's rats sometimes had the symptoms our mice displayed.

A meeting of the class was immediately convened and Dirk presented his case right down to an explanation of the reason the mice had scurvy to begin with. Apparently after watching their financial resources dwindle, the class had looked for a way save money on the cost of the vegetables and grain they had been feeding them.

One morning a boy come in with an ad for a brand of a popular dog food. The label on the bag read, "Everything Your Dog needs for Total Nutrition." At that time, with a 100-pound bag only costing $4.95, one of the boys did the math in great detail and proclaimed a hundred pounds of dog food would feed "a lot of mice for a long time." (Nothing like exact information for this class.) However, that had been good enough for the class, and dog food it was. The mice had a new diet. However, as the Poet Robert Burns once observed "The best schemes of mice and men often go awry," and apparently, awry their plans had gone.

However, the class learned a valuable lesson, that the digestive system of a vegetarian mouse had different needs entirely from that of a canine carnivore. What worked very well on dogs had proved to be devastatingly fatal to their horde of mice.

But, with mice dying all around them they went into crisis mode, deciding to see if feeding the mice green grass from the lawn in front of the school would work until a better plan could be put in place. I was afraid Wesley was going to have a stroke when he saw the bare spots in his front lawn, but the mice attacked the grass as surely as a man dying of hunger would attack a Big Mac. The results were nothing short of spectacular.

By the next morning most of the mice were looking better and had already started walking on the balls of their feet again (if mice have balls on their feet). By the second day no more mice had died, and soon life was back to normal in mousedom.

The kids never did find a laboratory willing to buy their mice. But out of the experience, they learned that mice purchased by laboratories were expensive due to the genetic breeding program they went through to make sure that all the mice were from the same pure genetic strain for their medical tests. I didn't know that at the time either. However, in true business fashion, they repositioned their product and found dozens of eager buyers in the students from other classes and schools who were willing to part with their allowance money to buy a pet white mouse. After all the publicity the white mice had gotten all year, it seemed every kid around wanted to get in on the action. So the kids paid off the original loan and had nearly $100 left over. Part of the money was spent on an end-of-the-year party and, frankly, I can't recall what they did with the balance.

However, I was to find out that apparently security must have been rather lax around the mouse house and we must have had some jail breaks. Several decades later I was asked to come back to the new Phoenix Elementary School to give a workshop on teaching resiliency to kids. As I was telling the story of the mouse house as an example of teaching life lessons, I saw one of their faces light up in a true "aha!" moment. About the time I was congratulating myself on getting my point across, she spoke up. It seemed she lived close by and had always wondered why the wild mice around Phoenix Elementary School were white instead of the normal gray. Now she knew the "Rest of the Story." I guess that legacy is better than no legacy at all.

Chapter 15

The Boy and the Box of Golden Oak

When a program is designed to help kids learn about themselves and their world, success can be measured in a different way. Here's the story of a little boy who didn't take a single test and did hardly any assignments during the year, but I considered his year a real success.

Mike came to the new class extremely introverted and shy. He wasn't a troublemaker and I don't think anyone had given up on him. He was just one of the "quiet ones" who sat in the back of the room or in a corner, hoping to go unnoticed. He didn't show much confidence in himself, and acted like he felt his opinion wasn't worth anything to anybody. To watch him grow during that year was pure magic. Many teachers might look at his year's work, consisting mostly of just one small oaken box and a few miscellaneous assignments, and not give him much of a grade, but in my book Mike gets an A+.

Early in the year, Mike came to school one morning with a dirty oil-stained little box and wanted to know if I thought he could refinish it. It was just after I had shown some of the class how to put a beautiful polyurethane finish on the new wooden chessboards they were making. Mike hadn't the courage to take on a project as grand as a chessboard, but now he came in apologetically with his greasy wood box, standing back from my desk like he was sure I wouldn't have time for him. Eventually he screwed up his courage, wondering whether his box could be finished "like the chessboards." He asked it like he was hoping I would say no.

The little box he held was like some of these kids. It might not look like much, but sometimes a scruffy lump of coal can hide a diamond in the rough. So I told Mike I thought it was an excellent choice, hoping there was something under the grime worth the effort of uncovering. With that blessing Mike seemed eager to begin and I sent him off to start the process with a toothbrush and some paint thinner.

The box had apparently been his grandfather's, who used it for leftover nuts and bolts from fifty years as an amateur mechanic. It certainly looked like there could have been fifty years of accumulated grease and grime on it. There was no way to know what type of wood was underneath all the grease. I really couldn't tell whether it would be worth all the work or not, until Mike cleaned it up and revealed just what was under the grime. At the time I didn't realize that the real value of this box wouldn't be in its wood, but what would happen to the boy in the process.

Mike spent a whole week working with steel wool, a toothbrush and paint thinner, and finally exposed a great little Golden Oak box hidden beneath all the dirt and grime.

It apparently had been part of an old roll-top desk, probably a letterbox because of its size, about 8 inches square and 3 inches deep. It had delicate inlaid brass hinges and a certain charm about it. And if my imagination wasn't playing tricks on me, I think Mike was already standing slightly taller as the others took notice of what he had. One boy even offered to buy the box from him but, unbeknownst to me, Mike had other plans.

Now, after thoroughly cleaning the box, Mike set out in earnest with sandpaper, beginning the process of preparing it for its polyurethane finish. It probably took him two or three weeks and a hundred questions before he had the courage to even consider working on the actual finishing process. He would work a spell and then cautiously approach my desk, standing behind anybody else who might be there as though he didn't feel his question was as important as the other kids'. Then, with a little encouragement, he would stammer out his question, which I would answer as best I could. He would go back to his workspace and I would watch him agonize over whether he was ready yet to apply the polyurethane or if he should work on it a little more.

With plenty of time and patience, there's nothing difficult about putting a furniture-grade finish on any piece of wood. All it takes is a little know-how and a lot of effort. Mike had the time and the patience to be exacting, and I began to wonder what he might be able to do with his little box. In a class where I was used to watching kids dive in, throw things together and get on to the next project, Mike had something else. I saw the other kids beginning to notice too. This was unique, and I began to realize how special this box and boy really were.

He would sand awhile and look at his box from all angles. Then he'd run his fingers lightly over the surface and gently use the fine sandpaper. It was as though he already had a picture in his mind of how his little box would look when he was done, and yet it was as if some part of him wasn't quite sure he could actually do it. Finally, almost a month into his project with untold hours of patient cleaning and sanding, he picked up the brush and dipped it in the can of finish.

When putting a finish on wood, the first few layers are applied to build up a base coat so one can carefully sand off the high spots, leaving the low parts of the surface untouched. Then new layers are added and left to dry, and the process is repeated. The trick is to stop sanding each layer at the just the right time, allowing the low spots to build up while again sanding off the high spots. Eventually, if this is done carefully, both the high and low areas of the surface can be brought to one even level which then can be finely worked into a glasslike surface.

Watching Mike learn this technique was a joy to behold. He would gently sand awhile, then run his fingertips over the surface, reading its highs and lows as he learned when to sand and when to stop. After months of careful sanding and feeling, sanding and feeling, then adding another layer of finish, he began to have confidence in his newfound ability. He seemed to know where he was going, and I thought he probably had what it took to get there.

Not many kids have the patience this process requires, at least not to begin with. They don't take the time to let the polyurethane really dry, or they don't have the patience to spend the hours it requires to carefully sand, re-coat, let dry and re-sand again. Mike did, and he also utilized all of his waiting and much of his work time to read and ponder. You can always tell when someone begins to really understand what they're doing, because they can sand with their hands, feeling the surface as they go and at the same time read a book or just think. Mike was getting pretty good at this. However, I couldn't help but wonder what he was thinking as he read and sanded, then sanded and read. I knew he was changing inside, just as the little box was changing outside. His progress on the box was becoming a metaphor for what was happening to him.

As he approached the stage where he was ready to put on the last mirror-like coats of finish on his box, I held my breath. These final four or five coats are worked with emery paper so fine that the surface begins to feel almost like satin as you reach the final stages. I still have in my mind a picture of Mike, sitting there working patiently on his little box, reading a book or listening to music or maybe just listening to what was happening around him. Slowly the box became an attention-getter. The more he worked on it, the more beautiful it became. The more beautiful the box became, the taller Mike stood.

The year Mike was in my class, we were beginning to have a steady stream of people coming through to observe the class in action. Somehow, word had gotten around about the unusual program at our school. There was rarely a day when there weren't a few students from one of the education classes at the college, or a cluster of new student teachers, observing. This was also the year Henry was being considered for the presidency of a new community college to be built, although we didn't know he was being observed at the time. In addition, there were always curious people from the community who heard about the strange things "that teacher" was doing at Phoenix Elementary and wanted to see him waste their tax dollars.

As people wandered through the clutter of old refrigerators, work tables strewn with half-done projects, and a few old sofas, Mike and his beautiful oaken box stood out like a jewel among the clutter. There were always comments or questions about his box or his work. The attention began to give Mike more courage, and sometimes he would even look people in the eye as he answered their questions. Occasionally I overheard him explaining just what he was doing at whatever step of the process he was in. I think it was beginning to dawn on Mike that he was doing something special, something other people felt might be impossible for them, and it is powerful when a child begins to feel he is special.

During the last month of school, Mike and his box were inseparable. He carried it with him to lunch. He carried it home at night and back in the morning. It gave me a lump in my throat to watch the change that had come over Mike as his little box began to take on a new life and beauty. I often wondered what his granddad thought of his bolt box and grandson now.

On the last day of school Mike came to my desk, holding his box shyly in both hands. For just this moment he was back to his tentative self. He set the box gently on my desk and in almost a whisper he said, "It's for you." At first I thought I heard wrong, but one look at his face and I knew that's what he'd said. I watched him for a few moments and said, "Mike, you can't do that. You have worked too hard to just give it away now." He stood there and looked me in the eye and with a small, shy smile simply said, "I was making it for you. It's for your chess pieces."

Once in a great while the fortunate among us receive a gift whose value is beyond estimate, a gift so humbling we can never forget it. Such a gift sits in front of me as I write this, right where it has been for the last forty years. It is a small box made of golden oak, painstakingly finished with untold layers of hand-rubbed finish, applied impeccably with hours and hours of loving care.

On the open market it might not be considered priceless, but to me it is, because I understand how much of a young boy's heart was put in that box. In all the years that have passed by, that little boy has never been further from my thoughts than his little box is from me now.

As I write this, there are tears in my eyes when I look at that simple but elegant oaken box sitting on the corner of my desk, still holding my chess pieces after all these years. It's still as beautiful as the boy who made it. Over the years I've never received a more heartfelt gift than the one Mike gave me that day. How many people would spend almost a year lovingly salvaging an old piece of junk, turning it into a work of art, and then so generously giving it away?

In the process of finalizing this book one of the class was finally able to find Mike. It has been many years and I had a lump in my throat as I dialed his number to express, to the now-grown man, what the box had meant to me. I wanted him to know how it had been, and still is, an inspiration to me to persevere in long, arduous tasks (like writing this book). Now that its presence had helped me so much in my life, it was time for me send it back to its creator.

Mike, I hope you still treasure this box, as much as I have, and I hope it will warm your heart now as it has mine over the years. Please accept it as a memento of the fine young boy who changed an old, nondescript box into something of beauty, and then made it all the more beautiful, by giving it away.

Mike and his Oak Box with friend.

Chapter 16

Ronnie Crosses the Big Divide

Finding the key to the lock is halfway home, and sometimes keeping the key secret is the other half of the equation.

With tears streaming down his face, a young boy sat in our Glasser Class Meeting, choking out his story about his previous treatment as a problem reader. It wasn't anything I hadn't heard a dozen times, but each time it bothered me a little more. It seems Ronnie had received the best help his well-educated teachers and reading specialists knew how to provide. He told of how he had been read to, how he had been asked to read aloud, how they tried workbooks and films, but as time went on the frustration levels increased in both parties. He was then kept in during recess, during the noon hour and after school for extra work. Still he couldn't read. Apparently other, more special techniques were resorted to. Ronnie sat there in the circle of his classmates and friends with a wet area growing in the front of his Levi's, as he told of being locked in closets and even trapped in a box placed under the teacher's desk, staying there for hours at a time because "he wasn't trying hard enough."

As I write this, I find myself realizing that these teachers were actually very good. They had just been pushed to their wits' end and in their mind it had become a battle of wills, the teachers' against a little boy's. Sadly in this situation, the boy can react in one of several ways. He can either believe there is something wrong with him or decide that he is just stupid and withdraw into himself. In some cases they may just get mad and resist the pressure, as this boy had. He hated reading. He hated the teachers who were forcing a hated subject on him. Any attempt at cooperation or effort went out the window. The result being, we now had a very nice little boy who still couldn't read as he sat in a sixth-grade classroom wetting his pants as he told the story. While I understood how frustrating it can be for the teacher, there is no excuse for what happens to many kids in this situation.

I still can't help wishing I could gather a few of Ronnie's reading specialists and some of my own grade school teachers from my past, and together he and I would teach them all how to use a new, unfamiliar computer and new software. First, we would have the best computers and the finest software. Then we would demonstrate how well the computers worked and how quick and easy they were to use, and how much they all would enjoy using them.

Then of course, Ronnie and I could "help" them. As they struggled we could stand behind them, pointing out on the screen just what they were doing wrong. We could tell them once again how easy it all is. If they didn't learn the basics quickly enough, we could always have an extra session for them during their coffee break or after class in the evening. If this didn't work, we could just stand over them and berate them for not "trying hard enough" or perhaps lock them in a closet for an hour or two so they could think about it. After all, if they would just try harder they would find out just how easy this new computer and program really was to operate.

Of course we all know this is ridiculous. In my experience there is one thing of which I'm certain. Three decades after buying my first Apple II computer and using probably ten or fifteen different computers over the years, having someone stand over the screen trying to help me doesn't do much but raise my blood pressure and theirs.

I believe any child is eager to learn to read when they first enter school. They come with such great expectations in all areas. However, the golden prize that outshines all others at that age is reading. What child doesn't love being read to? What child doesn't dream of being able to read as he watches his older siblings absorbed in a good book? If, by the sixth grade, a child is wetting his pants over difficulty with reading, someone has failed that student badly and I don't believe the child is ever the one to blame.

I think Ronnie somehow got started on a downward spiral of expectations, his and the teacher's, and both began to feel the pressure of failure. For him it would have been embarrassing to be singled out having trouble with something other kids were doing easily, and it probably just went downhill from there. By the time he reached the sixth grade, he wanted no part of reading, teachers or school. And while this particular boy is successful today, he still has no use for school or education in general and only reads when it is absolutely necessary for his business.

So in the sixth grade, Ronnie just stayed away from anything that smacked of reading. However, he actually enjoyed picking up a comic book and "looking at the pictures." And motorcycle magazines; Ronnie pored over them too. But as time went on, I noticed he spent what seemed to be a long time to be just looking at the pictures. One day when he was snacking on a bowl of cereal during reading time, I noticed he was, again, spending way too much time staring at the back of the box to be just looking at the pictures. However, in my classroom I didn't care what they were reading, be it comic books, cereal boxes, ads, or motorcycle magazines. It was not unusual to see boys and girls with the problem Ronnie had, poring over stacks of comic books during reading time. I know, I know, heresy!

In Ronnie's case, after six months of thumbing through comic books, motorcycle magazines and even instruction manuals (we never called any of this reading or they would start avoiding them too), I noticed Ronnie would go to the restroom and be gone for up to an hour at a time. I didn't think too much about it the first time. Then as it happened again, I began watching and noticed he was usually hiding a book as he went out the door. I thought I wouldn't say anything and see what developed.

One reason I cut Ronnie a little slack was because it took me back to my own childhood, when I would sneak out of class while the teacher droned on and on about some dreaded subject. I would head to the restroom with a book of Robert W. Service's ballads. I'm not sure where I picked up my love for poetry at that age, but I loved to read Robert W. Service ballads, and in the fifth or sixth grade, set out to commit to memory, first *The Cremation of Sam McGee* and then *The Shooting of Dan McGrew*, both by Service. Frankly, I couldn't think of a better use of my class time or a better place than the boys restroom at Murphy Elementary School to learn poetry. Unbeknownst to my dreaded teachers, poetry was to become a lifelong passion.

After a week or two of Ronnie's little sojourns, I thought it was time to find out what he was really up to. So the next time he left for the bathroom I waited a few minutes and moseyed out the door, down the hall and into the boys restroom. As I entered I could see Ronnie's shoes under the partition of one of the stalls, but his pants weren't down around his ankles and I knew I had him. So I casually entered the stall next to his, stood up on the toilet lid and peered over the partition. Just as I suspected! Ronnie was sitting on the closed toilet, hunched over his book and deeply immersed in the story. With a smile on my face I left the restroom and wandered back into the classroom. Apparently Ronnie had gained enough skill and had his curiosity piqued while reading his cereal boxes and comic books to expand his horizons. He had the skill, but not confidence yet to admit it, and his secret was safe with me.

I'm happy to report that by the end of the year Ronnie was openly reading and had really begun to blossom. He is now a successful businessman with a company of his own and happily married for nearly thirty years to the love of his life. He's a wonderful family man I count as one of my good friends to this day.

The twelve years in age difference that separated us then was as insignificant as it is now. When I signed on for duty with that ragtag group of kids, little did I realize I was signing up for a lifetime assignment and a number of enduring friendships.

Chapter 17

Grades 1 through 12 in 90 Days?

When I think of the three months I spent as a math instructor in the Army, I still feel cheated by my schooling.

Some of my ideas on how to reach kids were based on what hadn't worked for me during my twelve years in school. Then, after leaving high school, I went into the Army to avoid the whole problem. I wasn't expecting to learn anything earth-shattering about education while I was there, but I did. I was to have an experience that left me extremely regretful of my own wasted years of anger and frustration, now knowing there was a better way.

During my enlistment, as the number of draftees dwindled, the Army was looking for more recruits. One fact I had stumbled across while in the Army was that half the draftees called up for testing failed at the entry-level. It seems they couldn't pass a high school GED and their experiments at retraining dropouts, in an attempt to bring them up to the Army's minimum standards, were not successful.

However, the Army discovered another possible pool of draftees, and the initial experiment was rather encouraging. It seemed that countrywide there was a surprising number of people who, for whatever reason, had managed to avoid school altogether. The Army drafted

350 of these men who had never darkened a classroom door, and assumed they were illiterate. It was attempting to see how quickly these men could be brought to a level equivalent to those who graduated from high school. Apparently the difference between the dropout group and the ones who never went to school was one of attitude. These men were excited and eager to have a chance to go to school, something they had never done before. In contrast, the dropouts had been disinterested in anything that smacked of learning or school due to their own experience.

The University of Maryland had designed a program for the Army where people without any formal education could obtain a GED certificate in a relatively short time if they were interested. It was my good fortune to be at the Army base where a hundred or so of the original 350 men drafted for the experiment were to be trained. The University already had a training center at the base and I had been hanging around trying to build up my nerve to try some of their remedial programs. Then something happened that was to shape what I thought of education, and again probably changed my life.

I came to know the sergeant in charge of the center and, for some reason, he asked if I would be the math instructor for thirty of the men the Army had inducted. When I attempted to tell him that I wasn't qualified, he just said not to worry about it and besides, it would get me off the roster for KP and guard duty. That was good enough for me. What he knew that I didn't was that the instructor didn't have to know the subject. The material put together for this program would do the teaching. The instructor was only someone to sit in the classroom and hand out the material and keep an eye on the clock. For that, apparently I qualified.

The first surprise was how normal these supposedly illiterate men were. In general conversation and by all appearances, they were just like regular people I met in life. However, apparently the Government automatically assumed that anyone who had not attended school would be illiterate. By this arbitrary categorization, many of history's great thinkers and world changers, including some of the founders of our country, would be called "illiterate," which we know is not true.

The question was, were they illiterate or had they self-educated somewhere along the way?

The men seemed normal in all respects; maybe it was because they had listened to the news as they grew up, traveled and been part of the workplace. They weren't illiterate, as the Army had assumed; in fact, most of the men found the material relatively easy.

The next thing that surprised me was how simple and logical the material was and how it was presented. For the purposes of the program, the material and the way it worked was called Programmed Learning. In essence, the workbook would present a single piece of information in just a sentence or two. Then the next sentence would ask them a question about what they had just read. Whether they answered the question right or wrong determined which line (lines were all numbered) they went to next. If they got the answer wrong, they were directed to one number. If they got the answer right, they were given new information. So it went; a fact or two and a question, a new fact and a new question. Sometimes there was a picture and a question, sometimes a short story and a question. They worked their way through the material at their own individual pace, with plenty of breaks and no pressure, in a relaxed and congenial atmosphere. The men loved it and they spent their day encountering the success of a right answer every few sentences. And, if they missed a question, no big deal, the material they didn't quite grasp was presented again in a different way in their next section.

As the Sergeant had said, there was little for me to do but hand out the day's workbook, occasionally show a movie, and stand there looking wise. The fact that I wasn't qualified to teach math didn't matter because the subject matter wasn't dependent on me as a teacher. The material and the way it was arranged was the key. It was simple and direct and the men loved it. Was it because these men had something I had lost by the fifth grade? They believed learning was fun, exciting and interesting. The men didn't even want to quit at break time! But then, they hadn't been put through this same math day after boring day. Maybe that was why this program had little success when used on high school dropouts. They all hated school already and had resisted the whole idea from the very start. To them it was just more of the same old BS so they wouldn't give it a chance. And as we know, there are none so deaf as those who will not hear.

I worked with these men an hour a day, and the rest of the day they took other high school equivalency classes. As the days turned into weeks, probably what impressed me the most was the sheer excitement and enthusiasm they had for material that was rather basic.

As they went down the page or through the material, the questions would include not only what they had just been given, but a review of the material in the paragraph above, and sometimes there would be a question or two on material earlier in the presentation. The farther they went the more comprehensive the tests became, but it didn't seem to bother them. The magic seemed to happen because of the immediate need to repeat information they had just learned in the previous few minutes. Maybe that made it easier to remember later, because in a couple of minutes, they were asked to repeat it again. By the time they were asked to repeat it three or four times, it seemed like it was locked in their minds.

The results didn't surprise me. By the time we reached the end of the allotted time for the class, 92% of them passed. These men had conquered the equivalent of twelve years of math, while at the same time they were also studying a full range of other class material. They earned a high school GED diploma, covering grade 1 through 12, in just ninety days. I don't believe I have ever met a prouder bunch of GIs. They had just conquered a large personal dragon in a short period of time.

The men were normal in all respects; they had listened to the news as they grew up, traveled and been part of the workplace. They were not illiterate as the Army had assumed. In fact, most of the men found the material relatively easy. As these men were assimilated into the larger part of the Army, I know they felt really great about what they had accomplished.

At the same time I was left feeling cheated and conned. If these men could get a high school diploma in ninety days, it made me question the twelve years I had spent in dull, boring classes. When I thought of what I learned in my twelve years, I didn't seem to have anything these men didn't have, except a bad attitude and contempt for all my teachers.

In particular, those days also made me think of the hopelessly long year I spent in the despised fifth grade. For example, we had to learn the names of the states, their capitals, and how to spell them. When we had trouble, we were kept in at recess and noon hour to write long detention sentences. Now, many years later, I've noticed two things. First, I haven't worked the names of any capitals into a conversation since; and, second, I couldn't spell most of them when I left the fifth grade and can't spell them today.

However, in grade school, I did learn one thing that still sticks with me. I find geography dreadfully boring. Oh, intellectually, I know it probably isn't, but it's like going to the dentist. The dentist I went to as a child believed Novocaine was harmful for children so he wouldn't give it to anyone but an adult. So after having my teeth drilled without Novocaine, I put dentists and geography in the same category; something to be avoided at all costs.

Chapter 18

Teresa Tries It Again

Rooting for the underdog is always risky.

Someway Teresa and I made it through that first year, and she returned again to my room for her last year in grade school. In many ways the second year was better and a bond of trust between us occasionally began to show. But for reasons only she knew, I was still the enemy and I suspected her animosity toward me was because I was an adult male, another man who couldn't be trusted. Would that wall ever come down? If it didn't, I could understand why.

With a few exceptions, the thaw between us continued. She now was a regular participant in creative writing, and she continued to have an extraordinary way of putting anger and frustration on paper from some reservoir of feelings deep within her. Some days she would write and some days she would just sit. When she did write, she wrote with the same vengeance and anger that she had in the beginning, and she loved topics that gave her the most chance to vent her rage. So I kept feeding her edgy things to write about and she became one of the more popular writers in the class.

One day while I was helping her with a story in a rare teacher-pupil interaction, I made a major error. I made the mistake of saying, "You know, Teresa, someday you could write the great American novel."

She instantly became explosive and threw the book she was holding at me. Then she screamed, "You tell everybody that. You don't care about me or know anything about my life and how I live." And, with that, she ran from the room, gone for the day. I had to admit she was right. I didn't really know anything about her life and I knew if I was going to help her, I had to correct that. What I found out in the coming days added to the ache I carried for her.

For whatever reason, many days Teresa sat terrified in school, terrified that when she returned home there wouldn't be anyone there. What a load for a small girl to carry alone. Some days I was very aware that many of these kids needed more than I could offer; because all I could offer was maybe a little understanding, lots of encouragement and perhaps a little hope thrown in. But I didn't think encouragement was enough. How do you give a kid hope when they can't see hope anywhere in their future and when you aren't sure there is any.

Teresa seems happy today.

Chapter 19

The Inquisition

In retrospect, it still amazes me how fearful people can be of new ideas, and of our program when they heard about it!

During the years in which our experimental program was functional, we never had a single complaint about our class from the parents of the kids who were actually in the classroom. However, for some reason, it created an amazing amount of controversy in the community and among the parents of children in the other classrooms. Some of these other parents were openly hostile as the rumors circulated about what "Smith and his radical classroom" were up to.

But when they heard that I was teaching kids how to build their own personal radio that would let the children from little Phoenix, Oregon, listen to Radio Moscow, the pot really began to boil!

I had told the class somewhere along the way how, as a little boy, I had built a radio on which I could hear the BBC and Radio Moscow. Furthermore I related how I was amazed when I would hear one international news story on our local radio station, and then a very different version from the BBC and yet even a third version from Radio Moscow. Since this was during the Cold War, it was scary for them to think their children might be getting "brainwashed" by either the BBC or Radio Moscow. Most people at that time didn't own a radio that would pull in anything but the local stations, and television wasn't developed internationally as it is today. It came to a head with a delegation of concerned parents visiting Henry, complaining about me, and demanding he fire me.

Henry had come to me after school that evening telling me of the donnybrook I was creating, saying the only way to combat it was to face my accusers at an open public meeting. We talked about it and with no little concern, I agreed to the meeting and a date was set.

Before the meeting Henry had warned me that, while he would be there, we would come to the meeting separately and not talk together beforehand or afterwards. He felt it wouldn't be wise for the parents to see him apparently siding with me, as apparently most of the community didn't realize how involved Henry was with the program. I understood, and we agreed to meet somewhere else after the meeting to debrief.

So it was. I sat that evening in front of 25 or 30 angry townspeople, none of whom had children in my classroom but who were members of the community with very strong opinions, facing accusations based on rumor and innuendo. However, as the meeting progressed, it seemed that it wasn't just about Radio Moscow, as the topics ranged far and wide. Seemingly, "that" teacher who allowed students to chew gum in his classroom, also allowed them to pop and eat popcorn all during the day. But the worst was yet to come.

Apparently, I allowed my kids to listen to "The Beatles" on a hi-fi during class time. Also, they wanted to know if it was true, that the kids were even allowed to play marbles and have chess games during class time. Furthermore, did I allow them to play marbles for "keeps"?

Once this group got wound-up, some of the accusations were amazing. At that point, some of them even questioned my loyalty to the country and wondered if I was teaching sedition in their small town. But, at the bottom of it all was simply the fact that I was doing something radically different from what they had ever had experienced, and they were scared.

It was difficult to sit there and hear their allegations without defending myself, although I knew I had little choice but to listen, if I wanted this thing to blow over.

After the meeting, Henry and I got together and he felt the worst was behind us. As usual, he seemed to be right. The meeting went a long way towards pacifying the group, and we heard little about my being a communist after that, which is not to say that they, in any way, approved of what was going on in that "Mr. Smith's room." But at least, all was quiet on the Western Front.

Chapter 20

Teaching Problem Solving

It ain't what you don't know that stops you; it's what you know for sure that ain't so that really slows you down.—old folk wisdom

On one occasion, someone asked how I taught problem solving. Well, to be truthful I am not sure I know how to teach problem solving. However, I do know how to create an atmosphere in which kids learn the skill, and maybe that is all teaching really is. However, of all the skills we hoped our kids would take with them into life, the one of identifying and solving problems was probably the most important. If a person holds a general confidence that they can solve any problem they encounter, that belief and resiliency it fosters will take them far in life.

Unfortunately, while one can write a lesson that gives kids experience in solving problems out of a book, life doesn't work that way. Problems faced in life aren't all neatly laid out for us in a book. In life, problem identification is really the trick. Usually, the solution is rather straightforward. First, it must be distilled into a problem which can be solved. Unfortunately, problem identification and setting up the problem is a little more difficult to teach than simple problem solving, unless you know the trick.

Teaching problem identification is as much an attitude as anything else. Life in the classroom presents plenty of opportunities to teach the skill, regardless of curriculum requirements, if the teacher can get out of the way, and if they have the right mind set.

Here is a classic example of how one class spent several weeks identifying and then solving real-life problems. In addition, it was a beautiful thing to watch, and that was about all the teacher could do was watch, unless the teacher wanted to be the one doing the learning.

This sequence started out as most things in our program usually did. This problem appeared on the horizon as a minor annoyance, hardly worth thinking about. However, when properly ignored it grew into a proper problem, one we could see and identify and to the kids, one worth solving.

In a classroom like ours, real learning is exciting and usually a noisy business, and the issue of the noise we made was an ongoing problem. When it came up once again, I didn't give it much thought, I had other, bigger problems than a little noise. If Wesley got too cranky, we would deal with it then.

Soundproofing the room with egg cartons.

But, it didn't go away, and after a while, out of my concern for Wesley's rising levels of stress, I had him come to present "our growing problem" to the class. When he explained how this class was causing

Teaching Problem Solving

problems for the rooms above us, and how we would have to tone it down, or lose our freedoms to operate the way we did, it finally got their attention.

However, after Wesley left, the class chose to attack the situation in a way I hadn't anticipated. I was hoping his visit would enlist their cooperation in trying to keep the noise levels down. But no, they decided to treat it as a problem to solve and see what they could come up with. Soon, they were talking about ways to deaden the sounds, instead of trying to quiet our activities. But I let them dream on.

Later I realized that, if left to my own devices, I would have attempted to solve the wrong problem. I was always looking for a way to lower our noise levels. However, the kids identified a different problem, one of sound transmission. Their reasoning was that since the noise wasn't a problem to us, we just needed to figure out a way to stop transmitting it to other rooms. To that end, they started to look for a totally different solution than I would have.

Down came the egg cartons.

After school, that day, we had thirty minds and pairs of eyes looking for sound-abatement solutions, some way to soundproof our room.

And, the next morning one of the girls brought in an article her grandfather had given her from one of his do-it-yourself magazines. The article told how someone had used regular old-fashioned egg cartons attached to the walls and ceilings to soundproof a recording booth at a small radio station. In those days, egg cartons were made of papier-mâché instead of plastic, and apparently made good sound absorbers.

However, I was skeptical. I didn't think deadening the sound in the room would stop sound transmission through the ceiling and walls. But, I didn't say anything or the whole noise level issue would have become my problem, and I would have been the only one doing any learning from thereon.

Up go the egg cartons again.

Once they had a direction, they went into action. Measurements were made of all the surfaces that would need covering. Then, they carefully measured an egg carton, and they made more calculations. For most of the day, small groups debated about how to measure and then calculate the number of egg cartons needed. All in all, thousands of measurements were made and reams of paper use in calculations. In the end, their conclusion was that they needed about 3,000 egg cartons.

On hearing that, I secretly doubted there were that many egg cartons in the whole town. However, they made the decision. The class would collect egg cartons to cover the walls and ceilings of our classroom. Soon parents, grandparents, aunts and uncles, plus half the town were all saving egg cartons for Mr. Smith's classroom.

But again I was wrong, in no time the kids had collected nearly 3,000 egg cartons. Next, they began to attach them to the ceilings and walls with thumbtacks. And, as they progressed, a muffled, near silence slowly fell over the classroom and complaints from the other classrooms ceased. Everyone seemed happy with the kids' solution. The teachers upstairs were happy, and that meant Wesley was happy which meant I was happy. And the kids, they all felt they had really accomplished something; they felt powerful.

However, the calm and quiet was not to last. In a few days, the class received a visit from the fire marshal, who informed us that our use of egg cartons as a sound deadener created a fire hazard. It seems that word had gone out about our unorthodox approach to the sound problem. He went on to explain how papier-mâché was flammable, and, therefore, the egg cartons made the walls and ceilings flammable. He added that whenever he became aware of a fire code violation, it was his duty as the fire marshal to enforce the law. Yes, we were indeed in violation of the fire ordinance. He then produced a Cease and Desist Order which told us to remove the egg cartons immediately, or we all would face dire consequences.

So down came the egg cartons and up went the noise levels, and the complaints began again. However, undaunted, the class went back into problem solving mode. This time it was one of the boys' grandfathers who came up with an old book which said a mixture of powdered alum and borax, mixed with water, made a good fireproofing solution. Then it said that all we had to do was soak the egg carton in the solution and dry them. Both ingredients were inexpensive and readily available at the local hardware store. After a quick meeting, the class dipped into

Renegade Teacher

their bank account, and a runner went to the hardware store. Soon the kids had a sample of the two products with which to experiment. A dozen egg cartons were soaked and dried. So the next day, they set about lighting the egg cartons on fire, except they couldn't.

Soon the class had the fire marshal on the phone. Yes, he would be happy to come over. However, after the kids gave their demonstration, the fire marshal produced a blow-torch for his tests. The class had carefully soaked the egg cartons completely and dried them thoroughly, and it apparently worked to some degree, but a blowtorch?

However, the blowtorch had no luck in igniting them either. After much consultation with the principal, it was decided that they could put their fireproofed egg cartons back on the walls and ceiling, and once again, calm and quiet settled over Smith's classroom, but I don't think any of those kids ever viewed their problems quite the same way again.

This experience for me once again proved these kids were seeing solutions I would never have seen. I had a preconceived idea that the problem was the noise and the kids saw it as the transmission of the noise to where it wasn't wanted. They were right that the noise wasn't the problem, so I would never have investigated what was a simple, elegant solution.

Since then, I have become aware that many new, creative solutions to problems in a given field come from people outside that field, simply because outsiders don't always know what won't work. However, experts in the field usually are well informed, whether right or wrong, on what conventional wisdom says won't work. This leaves the outsider to sometimes see simple solutions to so-called insolvable problems.

Chapter 21

Chess Ladder and State Tournament

What they learned about cooperative thinking not only pitted them against Henry in a chess showdown, it then took them to the top of the state high school chess championship. Not bad, for sixth-graders.

When one sees the classroom as a reflection of life and resolves to teach children about life and not subject matter, things evolve in a different way and serendipity seemed to have a hand in what went on. I can't recall how the game of chess became part of the warp and woof of our classroom, but I know that Henry's love of chess certainly played a part in it all. I had played chess when I was in the Army and had a hankering to make an inlaid wooden chessboard so, true to fashion, somehow it got to be a project I was going to help a couple of boys with. When they were finished, of course they wanted to know how to play the game, and it just took on a life of its own.

First it was just a chessboard. Then it was several. One day, the winner of a game which lasted several days put his name on the chalkboard to declare his victory. Then someone challenged him by putting his name below the first. Then another name appeared below the second, declaring their desire to play the winner of the pair above them. Soon there was a list of names, all in due course playing the person listed above their own. One chess ladder became two and two became three. Then someone liberated one of the plywood boxes that held basketballs in the gym. It made a perfect chess table when turned upside down. Soon another ball box made its way into our classroom. The janitor mumbled—he mumbled a lot over our classroom—and made another ball box. And, finally there were seven chess tables, with seven chess ladders and seven chessboards in full swing most of the time.

In Smith's room, chess was considered a worthy learning experience and a good brain exercise. There was another chessboard where an ongoing game of chess was played between Henry and three or four of the best players in the room. Each move was written on a piece of paper and hand-carried by a courier to his office, where he had an identical board set up and played his half of the game. When he figured out

Drawing a chess board on a ball box.

his next move, we would receive a call from his office, and the courier would run across the field separating the grade school from the district administrative office to retrieve his latest move. These were pitched battles, with Henry often expressing surprise at how this motley crew could collectively play an extremely good game. These battles were followed by the entire class, move by move. I'm not sure who got more of a kick out of these battles, Henry or the kids.

One day in the heat of battle, his king and consequently the entire game was at stake. The whole classroom had come to a standstill as they ganged up to defeat Henry. After an extended discussion weighing the various possibilities, a move was decided on. The courier was dispatched and Henry's response was eagerly awaited.

The result of the move was not what either side expected. It seemed that Henry had set up a classic chess trap for which the class had fallen. That evening, Henry came over and told me what happened. He said when the girl who was acting as courier came into his office, she looked like the cat that ate the canary. Henry, busy at the moment, quickly looked at their move, seeing they had gone for his trap, quickly wrote and made his move on his board, which left the class in an impossible position. When the girl saw his new move she broke into tears and ran from the room. Later he told me he felt like the Grinch who stole Christmas. He continued, saying he never would have pressed them that hard, except he had become used to their "take no prisoners" style of playing and had forgotten he was playing with fifth graders.

After a few months of watching them develop their skills on the chessboard, Henry came to me with a proposition. The county chess

A couple of boys from the chess team.

Renegade Teacher

tournament for high school students was to be held that month. He said he could get my team into the tournament as long as we understood it would just be for the experience, since only older entrants were permitted. They would be entered in the pool and play through the entire field, but they couldn't compete to win; it would be just for practice. So the four top chess players from Smith's room attended the tournament.

By Sunday afternoon, the weekend of the tournament, while the winning trophies were handed out to a high school team, it must have been a hollow victory; because there on the scoreboard for all to see was the Phoenix Elementary School team, ahead in total points. They came to school Monday morning beaming. But Henry wasn't finished. He next arranged for the same practice entry in the state high school chess tournament, to be held in Portland later in the spring.

On the appointed weekend, off to Portland went our little team, consisting of one 11-year old girl, a couple of tousle-headed boys and "Iron Mike," a boy I had inherited from, what his record called, an MR (as in mentally retarded) program in California. I can assure you, he was in no way mentally handicapped. However, as in many such cases, I don't think he knew this. He struggled because he did have a speech impediment and struggled to communicate. But, oh how he loved chess. He didn't need words to play chess and was getting pretty good at it, good enough to be one of the best four in the room. At the state tournament, he showed just how good he really was.

Well, you probably guessed it. When the tournament was over, again the fifth and sixth grade team from Smith's room had outscored the state high school chess champions. But the only trophy they brought home was a small inexpensive plastic one, about eight inches tall which the team found somewhere and had engraved with "Smith." It probably only cost a few dollars, but till today it remains one of my most prized possessions.

That next Monday those four kids came to school walking tall, but the tallest of them all was my refugee from California, Iron Mike. He had a grin that he just couldn't get off his face all day long. Henry came over to congratulate the class and, as an aside to me, said, "Now maybe you will get a little more respect in the teacher's room." Wrong! The only comment ever mentioned in my presence was, "It's not surprising they have done well. All they ever do in your room is play chess."

Chess was played everywhere by everybody.

Chapter 22

Teresa Moves On

Sometimes before they can come home, they have to go away. But would that little waif of a girl survive where she was going?

The next year, Teresa went on to the seventh grade, and a decision was made by the school authorities to incorporate her into the mainstream junior high program. Every week or so she would come back as a regular visitor to my classroom after school. By now I knew what she wanted. She wanted to be told once again, "You can do it, Teresa. It's all up to you."

This went on for most of her seventh grade year. Then one day, she just stopped coming. Later, I found out from some of the other kids that one noon hour she just got onto a motorcycle behind some biker who had been a familiar sight at the school, and rode off. Word was that they had gone to San Francisco to be part of a summer of love, among other things. I wondered whether Teresa would survive.

That first summer after she left, I wondered whether I would ever see Teresa again. There were some qualities about her that I would miss; that indomitable spirit; the fire with which she faced all adversities; that unstoppable soul. However, I doubted these were enough in her case.

Later that summer, Teresa showed up at the doorstep of my home, something that was to become a semi-annual ritual. I knew she hadn't come for idle conversation. It was always the same. What she really wanted was to hear those words again.

"You can do it, Teresa. Nobody else can do it for you. I know you were given a raw deal as a little girl, but it's all up to you now. From here on, you are the only one who can do it. We can never change the past, but what you do with the present and future is all up to you."

I couldn't help but wonder what would have become of Teresa if she had won the parent lottery like some other girls. To what heights would she have soared; what would she have achieved in her life if she had gotten all the breaks instead of adversities?

Teresa talks me into something.

Chapter 23

The Itinerant Flute Maker

Sometimes you just have to roll the dice and see what turns up. When working with a class like this, having good luck is always handy.

One morning in the late 60s at the very beginning of the "summer of love," one of the kids excitedly reported that he saw a real "hippie" the previous night. Everyone had heard the term but at this early stage of the movement, no one was sure just what the term meant, including me. But it was as though he was reporting the sight of Bigfoot or a flying saucer, and it really triggered the imagination of the class.

I realize now that probably no self-respecting flower child ever admitted to being a hippie as it was generally a derogatory label, coined for anyone with long hair, including rednecks and thugs who grew their hair long to hide who they really were. However, this boy had seen "one" and, to my consternation, invited him to come and visit our class. He reported having told the hippie that, "Mr. Smith won't mind; he's cool." Of course, not knowing exactly who or what this person was, I perhaps wasn't as cool with the idea as the kid thought I would be. I also knew that Wesley wouldn't be cool with the idea at all. As you may have gathered by now, Wesley wasn't one of the most broadminded people I knew. But the class was clamoring for action.

At this point I decided that after school I would take my little "hippie spotter" and we would go and meet this "hippie" before he made any visits to the school. I was about to announce my plans to the class when I was further informed that our potential new friend would be here in about twenty minutes. Well, that took care of that. True to his word, our new, rather colorfully dressed friend was punctual and showed up right on schedule.

As it turned out, we were in for a surprise. When the boy introduced him to the class as a "hippie," he replied, saying he was actually an itinerant flute maker. (A what? I wondered if Wesley would feel better now?) However, indeed he had a leather sack slung around one shoulder full of pieces of bamboo and bamboo flutes he had made. He then proceeded to sit on the carpet and start playing a flute.

The next hour or so was fascinating. After playing for some time, he took out a length of plain bamboo and showed us how he made a flute. Then he asked one of the class members to be the first to play on his new creation. The kids were captivated, and he promised to teach them all how to make their own flute. It wasn't long until I was totally comfortable with our new friend. The kids had dozens of questions about how he lived and how he viewed the world. After about an hour, he politely said he had to leave. He added that he would come back if I wanted him to, and also told me how to get in touch with him.

The front door of the school had hardly closed behind our new friend before I was sitting in Wesley's office. He was steaming! I don't know what buttons the guest had pushed, but in Wesley's mind I had invited a monster into my classroom, exposing my innocent, naïve children to who knows what. It was as if their mortal souls were now in danger.

I did my best to assure Wesley that I believed this earnest young man was perfectly harmless and seemed to be a man of character. Wesley didn't know what to say to that. After I had Wesley backpedaling a bit, I announced that I had invited our new friend back. Once again, Wesley was less than pleased with me when I left.

True to his word, our hippie returned and became another intermittent visitor to our classroom. Sometimes he would show up unannounced, and sometimes he would send word with one of the kids in advance. He worked with the children making flutes and teaching them how to play them. He added color and life to the room and for the duration of my term at Phoenix Elementary, he visited off and on every year.

In summer, our new flute maker seemed to live outdoors amongst the woods, which were plentiful around southern Oregon. I would occasionally run into him as he played and sold his flutes to theatergoers on the streets of Ashland. Eventually he settled down there and began making stained glass windows to supplement the line of flutes that he sold.

As the years went by, I became a regular purchaser of his stained glass windows. They flank the front doors of my home. I added them to some law offices I built, and used them in a small shopping plaza later. When I built Lithia Springs Inn I used a few, and there is still one over the door in the library. I'm always happy to find a new friend anywhere and I didn't have a single flute maker among the bunch.

These days, he plays great piano during the dinner hour at my favorite restaurant, the "Arbor House," just a couple of miles from the Inn. I've been eating there for over thirty years now, and they still prepare everything from scratch for each person. The Arbor House is the most caring, heartfelt restaurant I have ever had the pleasure of enjoying. To have my old friend (and favorite flute maker) play there is about as good as it gets.

Chapter 24

The Impossible Saltwater Aquarium

Using experiential teachings, you may not be quite sure what they'll learn, but you can be sure they'll learn something; usually far more than in any other way.

One summer, I taught a special summer program for the able and gifted at the college in Ashland. I was excited about the prospect and looked forward to working with an advanced group from all over the region. The first surprise was that they were no quicker at grasping concepts than my ragtag bunch of misfits back at Phoenix Elementary. Indeed, they weren't nearly as good at independent study and research as my own class, who were so often sent to me as problem kids.

However, we had a great summer, doing a project I had wanted to try anyway. It needed to be exciting for a bunch of accelerated kids who were used to advanced programs. In the end, I settled on a project in oceanography created from an idea which originated in a classroom at Phoenix Elementary. On one occasion the kids got into a discussion on what would happen if you put saltwater fish in fresh water, or vice versa. They came to the conclusion, after a little research in the library, that the fish would die if moved from one to the other. But this class was never one to let sleeping dogs lie, and a legitimate question had been raised. Might the fish live if you made the transition gradually enough, with just a bit of salt at a time? Good question.

I didn't know the answer to that question, but I thought it might be a great summer project. So I went to the biology department at the college and posed the question to the professors. If it were done gradually, would the fish survive? It seemed to be the unanimous opinion of these learned biologists that it was impossible for the average saltwater fish to adapt to fresh water. Only certain species like salmon could make that migration and it's journey, which sometimes killed even them, and they all died in the end.

In the case of a summer school project, in a way it really didn't matter what the outcome of the experiment was (except maybe to the fish), learning would happen either way. I was willing to bet anything that the kids would love doing the experiment. So arrangements were made. In the first week or so of summer school, we would take a field trip to the Oregon coast to bring back seawater and saltwater fish or whatever creatures we could capture.

Looking back on it all, I'm not sure whether it was legal to displace fish from their natural habitat or not; today it certainly wouldn't be. But in those days, there wasn't as much environmental awareness as there is today.

The class was then challenged to figure out the rate at which they would have to make the switch. We had all summer to change the water in the aquarium from salt water to fresh, and back again. Each day, the salt water would be diluted so that by midsummer, it was basically fresh water. Then the process would be reversed.

Since that summer, I have wondered whether we weren't being rather rough on the marine life. Each time when they changed the saline content it would affect the fish, some more than others. On many occasions our fish would start swimming on their sides or sink to the bottom. Then, most of them would be upright and swimming again by the next day. By the end of the summer, a goodly number of sea animals had survived the ordeal. They had made the transition from seawater to fresh and back again to seawater, and lived to tell about it.

At the end, the kids took home detailed notebooks, most of them ornately decorated, crammed with calculations and notes on fish species. They had noted what had survived the best and which fared the worst. Everyone involved had a good time, and all left feeling like real scientists. In addition, I think they learned something. Furthermore, I hope one thing they learned; don't always trust the advice of "the experts."

Chapter 25

The Worst Speller in the Class

Almost anything can be turned into a learning experience if you're more interested in teaching life skills than content.

Well, I guess it's time to let the cat out of the bag. It's time to admit to the class, some forty years later, that I was an impostor. For example, when I wrote on the blackboard, the kids knew I would "purposely" misspell every other word. It was their job to catch my errors, and they got very good at it. It didn't seem to matter what word I put on the board, someone would notice if it was incorrectly spelled. It soon became difficult to find a word that nobody could spell. Sure, some were better than others, but by the middle of the year everyone got into the act and it was hard to sneak anything by that bunch of eagle eyes. That is, all but one poor soul. He couldn't spell anything. And it seemed as the year went by, he didn't improve one bit. For all the five years I taught, I saw very little improvement in his spelling.

I'm sure some of the kids picked up on the fact that I was by far the worst speller in the class. As I write this, it's still amazing how many simple four and five-letter words that I have been using all my life still come out wrong. Anyone who has the spelling gene never understands. For those of you who didn't get it, I share your pain. My wife was not a native-born English speaker, yet rarely runs into a word she cannot just naturally spell. I have one daughter who has the spelling gene and another who is just an average speller. But she's still far ahead of me. I not only didn't get any spelling genes, I didn't even get the box the genes came in.

Spelling and a few other quirky handicaps served me well in those days as a teacher. When the kids sense that collectively they are better at many tasks and smarter in many areas than the teacher, it opens up the child's world. If an atmosphere is developed where it's OK to be wrong part of the time, truly amazing things happen. It gives them the courage to tackle problems they might otherwise avoid.

Kids thrive when they discover they aren't dependent on their teacher for their learning, and develop the courage to move beyond their level of comfort. Henry coined a label to describe what our overall goal was with these kids. We talked about resiliency, lifelong learning, deductive thinking and a variety of other concepts. But one day he asked me, "What happens when you throw a cat up in the air?" Instinctively I replied, "It lands on its feet." Then Henry said, "That's exactly what we need to do with these kids; give them the skills needed to land on their feet, regardless of what life throws at them. We need to teach cat-ability."

It was already evident that at least half the children who came to my classroom would not be employable in the technological society clearly visible ahead. Unless something happened to intervene, many of these kids were in trouble. It wasn't that they weren't smart enough, after all they had self-taught themselves a language before they came to school. But, for some reason they were missing the boat educationally.

In general, schools weren't teaching the skills and attitudes that would allow our students to thrive in whatever future that unfolds. So in this classroom we had thrown out the then-traditional curriculum, and in non-educational terms, we were attempting to teach "cat-ability." When you didn't have to stick to the curriculum's content, all sorts of things became tools for teaching reasoning, creative and deductive thinking and other skills needed to survive in an ever more complicated world.

I admit, and it may not have been exactly cricket, but I played a few tricks other than spelling on the class. I would shamelessly exploit any chance to create curiosity in a kid, or a bunch of kids, as I felt nothing drives thinking, problem solving and learning like a healthy curiosity. If we were going to teach these children resilience and how to solve life's little problems as they come up, stimulating natural curiosity was of paramount importance.

Once, I made a New Year's resolution to drop ten pounds and there was a scale in the teacher's room. One day, I came back after a break and without thinking wrote WOC 153 in small letters on the corner of the blackboard. My intention was to keep track of my weight loss for my own purposes and had no other motives. The next day I wrote WOC 152, and each day added to the list. Some days the number would go up and some days it would go down, but it was generally trending down.

I should have realized I couldn't slip everything past 30 sets of eagle eyes. It took only a few days until one of my quicker students, Jan Dunford, wanted to know what WOC 147 meant. Of course I wouldn't tell her. That drove her, and eventually most of the rest of the class, crazy. It finally got to the point where I was almost embarrassed to admit it wasn't any big deal and that I was just keeping track of what I weighed. But there was a lot of good head-scratching going on, so I let it run.

To keep it going, I even kept changing it. Just to add fuel to the fire and throw the kids off track, some days it would say WOJ 145 instead of WOC 145. That of course stood for, "without jacket" instead of "without coat."

All sorts of wild and crazy theories were proposed. Interest in it ebbed and flowed through the spring, but it was never too far from the surface. Finally at the end of the year, I broke down and admitted what this code stood for. I truly feared for my life. I rarely see Jan now, forty years later, that she doesn't remind me of that.

While this sort of game might be difficult to defend as educational, of one aspect I am sure: anything that makes the teacher human and reachable at a gut level enhances the learning process.

I didn't want the kids to respect me because I wore a necktie, or allowed or didn't allow them to chew gum in class. What we sometimes think of as respect is many times fear of authority. Instead, I feel the relationship with the student is most conducive to learning and preparing for later life if it is one of mutual respect and trust. In this state of mind, they can gain confidence in themselves and begin to realize that in many ways, they are equal or superior to their teacher. I wanted them to be able to say to themselves, "Hey, I'm just as good as Smith, and maybe even better in some ways."

Boys and some of their projects.

Chapter 26

You Win Some

Sometimes I wondered why some of them weren't in worse shape than they were.

The boy was about 11 or 12 years old, slightly built and a little over five feet tall. He had a leather harness around his chest and shoulders, attached to a leather strap held by a woman I assumed to be his mother. As if this wasn't bad enough, in her other hand she held a black umbrella with a pointed end. If the boy got to the end of the tether, she would yank on it and pull him back. If the boy drew too close to her, she would poke with the point of the umbrella. And so the dance went. The boy was old enough to be self-conscious about what was happening, but it seemed he had resigned himself to it. And, that apparently, was her way of controlling a 12 year old in a crowd.

It had been a beautiful Saturday afternoon, and I was at a farm auction with about a hundred other people. I had been enjoying the auction, the crowd, and a good, old-fashioned hotdog, until I saw the boy. Several others were apparently bothered by it also, but there didn't seem to be much any of us could do about it 35 years ago. I'm not sure if there's anything that anyone could do about it even today.

I suddenly lost my appetite for the hotdog and the auction, but as I drove away I couldn't put what I'd seen out of my mind. I just couldn't help but wonder what this was doing to the psyche of the boy and what else might be happening at home, behind closed doors. I also wondered what sort of behavior problems this treatment by his mother might cause and, as it sometimes happens, I was to find out soon.

A week or so later, the Principal came to my room asking if I could take "another one." Apparently, this boy was removed from two other area schools, for threatening a teacher with a knife, and I was his last chance. When I said yes, bring him in, it took me a minute to place him. Then, as I reflected back on what I had seen at the auction, I could only wonder how this would all unfold.

George at first seemed like a sweet, likable little boy with none of the anger issues I would have expected. But I held my breath. Our class was usually a pretty tolerant group. I suppose that was because a large part of them had one or another problem themselves. We worked a lot on tolerance in our Glasser Class Meetings, which gave us a great tool for working out issues. The first few days with George seemed to go reasonably well, until I started hearing from a few of the class members.

It seemed George had a habit that bugged some of the kids. His idea of being friendly was to stand within a foot or so when he talked with you. Most of us are more comfortable at two or three feet. One girl reported that George not only stood too close as he talked, but reached out and fingered her earring while carrying on a normal conversation in his silky, too-sweet voice. Hmmm.

More stories began to trickle in and I wasn't sure I knew how to handle the situation. He hadn't actually done anything wrong that I could put my finger on. He was just being creepy, as one of the girls called his behavior. Of course, it would have been easy to project his behavior ahead and imagine all sorts of inappropriate actions. The fact was that all he was doing was being weird, at least until a few days later.

On that particular morning just after the early recess, one of the kids came running into the classroom, out of breath saying, "Help, the librarian needs you. It's George. He has Mrs. Olse and Sharon penned in the corner, and has a pair of scissors."

The library was only about fifty feet down the hall, and I went running. When I arrived, George did indeed have the librarian and Sharon penned in the corner, holding them trapped behind a library table, brandishing a large pair of sharp pointed scissors.

I grabbed George, and pulled him back from the table and then made sure no one was hurt. Of course, today we would have to call the police, who would have arrested George and taken him away in handcuffs. The incident would be on the national news with the whole country wringing their hands, wondering what this world was coming to. Today it might seem odd that this wasn't done, but I'm glad it worked out as it did.

We sent George home for a couple of days, giving our class a chance to think things over and make a choice. Naturally someone called for a Glasser Class Meeting. At first, it seemed the whole group had run out of patience with George and were calling for his removal from our class. There was genuine fear, not of George, but because the reflection on our class might cause us to lose some of our hard-won privileges, all because of one bad apple. Then someone brought up what might happen to George if our class rejected him and the school refused him a place here. I was again amazed how intelligent, caring and creative thirty kids can be collectively, once they get in the mode of operating as a close knit team, thanks to Dr. Glasser.

I had told them the story of George, the umbrella and his mother earlier in his tenure with us. They were the ones who had to deal with George and I felt they needed to know what George dealt with at home. I am sure I would be fired today for divulging such information.

Now we were talking again about George's future, and that did it. Soon a consensus developed, George needed our help, not our rejection. Indeed, a few of the kids insisted that George would do almost anything to be able to stay with us, if given a chance. At the time, I wondered how much of this was a projection of their own need to be accepted by the class, but that didn't matter.

It was proposed to banish George from the classroom and make some reasonable rules for his behavior and how he could earn his future return to the group. They would explain to George in a Glasser Class Meeting just what he was doing that made them uncomfortable, and that if he could change some of those habits, they would welcome him back into the class. Of course this wouldn't have worked had it come from the teacher. But since it was coming from the very kids he wanted to be accepted by, I thought it might work out. We would see.

Renegade Teacher

There was an empty classroom next to our room that was used occasionally for shop work and larger projects. The kids suggested it could be George's new "detention center" except during our structured class time, when he would be with the class. The rest of the time, while we were working on our projects and in groups, which was most of the time, he would be outside the classroom, until he could earn his way back.

Immediately George wanted to come back into the classroom so badly, he would creep up and stare through the window in the classroom door, standing there by the hour forlornly watching the class. At that point, the class decided to put newspaper over the window so he couldn't see us. This, drove George nuts, and it became obvious that shunning someone could be a powerful motivator. I began to realize the class might be right. George was going to do whatever it took to be back in our class. It also occurred to me that I might have a new tool in my arsenal. Make school voluntary and make sure class is so desirable that children want to be there, then make class attendance subject to good behavior. I say this tongue-in-cheek; however, I knew from experience the kids in this type of classroom wouldn't even stay home when they were sick.

Soon George was coming back for short durations at first and eventually full time. I'm not saying that we didn't have any more issues with him, particularly at first, but by the end of the year he had integrated into the class as well as many of the other kids. The following year he even survived the regular junior high program.

I hadn't heard the last of George. One evening after school, a year after he left, he showed up in the classroom with a cherub-like grin on his face. He was holding an Excedrin tablet, a full two feet across, one that he had made out of papier-mâché in an art class. He gave it to me, saying I deserved it for all the headaches he had given me. I kept that Excedrin tablet around my room for the rest of my tenure there.

After a couple of years, I lost track of George. Then one of the teachers brought a newspaper article about him becoming an Eagle Scout. Indeed, kids never cease to amaze me. Not only did George amaze me, the kids in the class had the compassion and vision to do what they would want to have happen to them. I think they gained as much insight into their own lives as did George. Now 40 years later, I would like to meet him again.

Chapter 27

Life, Death and the Sears Catalog

The key to reaching kids is to give them something real to work with, even if it's just a Sears & Roebuck catalog then, or eBay or Amazon now.

When I look back at my short tenure as a teacher, a few experiences really stand out. When a teacher opts to teach children about life, not subject matter, finding meaningful experiences can be particularly challenging, at first. However, once you get the hang of it, it's not really that difficult. One of the tried-and-true exercises in my bag of tricks was teaching life skills from the Sears & Roebuck catalog. I stumbled onto this idea rather innocently but, in retrospect, most of my good ideas started that way. This one actually came from kids who were an endless source of many things we did.

One morning the kids came to school all abuzz about a plane crash that was on the news. What made this crash so captivating and unique was the inability of the rescue teams to get in to the crash site. A small airliner had crashed north of Nome, Alaska, 150 miles from civilization. Bad weather and the fact that there was nowhere to land around the crash site left them stranded. Nobody knew whether they were even alive at that point. So we began to monitor the story as it unfolded on our old black-and-white TV and their crystal radios.

The news stories were all about whether the crash victims would be reached in time, and what the rescuers might find when they finally got there. That day our Glasser Class Meeting was all about the crash, and once they got started on the topic there was no getting them on to other things. So we just went with it. Whenever I had a bunch of kids excited about something, it was all about using the opportunity. Now I just had to figure out how to channel that energy.

It wasn't long before I realized this could be a great opportunity to teach critical thinking and value judgment. Off the cuff I started posing questions such as: "If you were the captain of the rescue team, what would be important to take with you, bandages or food; water or kerosene heaters?" So it went, with the debates raging back and forth from the ridiculous to the sublime.

A rescue team makes plans.

During the morning recess I jotted down a few ideas, went to the office and made copies of them while the kids were gone. By the time they got back I had a worksheet for them, which was the beginning of what became a mainstay of many a good learning experience.

I had them break into groups of five. Each group became a "Strategic Crash Rescue Team," with the teams designated as Team Alpha, Team Bravo, Team Charlie, etc. Then I gave them my best impression of a "Mission: Impossible" kickoff.

"Your mission, should you choose to accept it, is to plan and mount a rescue effort to reach 53 people in a downed aircraft north of Nome, Alaska. Your information packet is now being distributed. You have 24 hours to prepare your rescue plan and be ready to leave for the crash site immediately thereafter."

For this exercise, each rescue team would be provided with a Tucker Sno-Cat, with an assumed load limit of 2,000 pounds. In addition, each team would have a working budget of $7,000. It was the team's responsibility to determine what supplies they would take and the amount of each item. They would decide whether they needed food or medicine, gas or blankets. I reminded them it was a 150 mile trip each way, and they would be judged on their decisions concerning what they took or didn't take.

The teams would make their plans, calculate the load they could carry given the load limits of their vehicle, and decide what to take with them while staying within their monetary budget and load limits. They were told they would have until 2:00 the following day to make their plans and prepare for their presentation to the Crash Review Committee, which was the entire class. The committee would listen to their plan, then decide whether the crash victims had survived or perished. This proved to be pretty heady stuff for fifth and sixth graders.

I had never seen a class so motivated and excited, so eager to begin. Most worked right through the noon hour and some worked through afternoon recess as well. A few even stayed after school, and I imagine some of the class didn't sleep much that night. Ah, the power of experiential education!

---

[1] Tucker Sno-Cats were early all-terrain vehicles the kids were familiar with from reading old National Geographic magazines about Sir Hillary's assault on Mt. Everest and about early expeditions to the South Pole. Tucker Sno-Cat was made a few miles from the school and added a level of believability to this exercise.

They appeared again early the next morning. Some worked again through the morning and noon recess. Some even brought their own sack lunch so they could eat at their desks while they worked. By 2:00 only a few teams were really ready to make a presentation and I could see good stuff was happening in the groups. So, after warning them that people may be dying up on the mountain, an extension was granted.

When the first presentation was made, the Crash Review Committee declared all the victims deceased. This team had forgotten to figure their own weight in their load calculations and had to throw most of their supplies out because they exceeded their weight limits. One of the other teams, made up mostly of boys, had all of their victims declared dead because they had taken too much food and candy bars and ended up short on medical supplies for the victims.

One of the main problems that appeared in this first exercise was arguments over what the different items cost and their weight. Luckily there was one old Sears catalog in the room. One team was quick to claim it as an infallible reference source. This impressed the Crash Review Committee and when we did the next such exercise, many homes in our little town were suddenly without Sears & Roebuck or Montgomery Ward catalogs.

Today if I were using this type of exercise in a classroom, I would simply adapt it to the computer and internet. In fact, I would love to work with a computer gaming company devising a game like this for teaching critical thinking. So, if you have an in with a computer gaming company that is looking ahead to the market schools will present in the future, tell them to come visit me.

Needless to say it wasn't long before Providence (moi, in this case) provided a major train wreck in the snow-choked mountains between our school and the Oregon coast. Since there are no roads in or out of this area, they were all debating chainsaws or no chainsaws, mountain gear or not. They were all adding, subtracting, balancing, judging and debating whether to take this or that, what to throw away and what to keep. About the time they were all in high gear, Providence (me again) declared that everybody's vehicle just broke a spring on the suspension, requiring them to throw away fifty pounds' worth of their supplies. You could hear the howls a block away. But, it was this type of element that made it so interesting for them and always created another wave of critical thinking, value judgments and calculations.

Had I told them to stop and get their math books out (which we didn't have) and do the story problems, I would have been tarred, feathered and run out of town on a rail. In addition to their thoroughly enjoying the scenarios, I never would have gotten this quantity or quality of work out of them using a book. In addition, they were working with all the judgment calls and critical thinking that was part of real life. This was almost as exciting for the class as real-life experience, such as raising laboratory mice or building radios to sell.

The class never tired of these exercises in one form or another. All I had to do was come up with a bigger, more outrageous catastrophe than the last, and they were off and running. While we continued to do major "rescues" using every new catastrophe I could devise, this type of learning experience was far more popular than expected.

One noon hour, a trio of girls approached me, asking for a Sears Catalog mission for the three of them. Flying by the seat of my pants (you do a lot of that in this kind of program), and knowing these girls were a little bit horse crazy, within a few minutes I gave them some verbal instructions. They would be moving to Montana together and opening a tack shop for horse paraphernalia in Bozeman. I would supply them with an old pickup that would carry the three of them, along with a 1,000 pound load.

They would have a budget of $5,000 to purchase inventory for their tack shop and buy gas, food and lodging along the way. "Oh, and don't forget your first month's rent when you get there." I told them I wanted to see their order form with calculations and budget as soon as they had it ready.

The three of them worked nonstop through the week and were back on Monday morning debating about whether they had planned for enough gasoline or too much. Sometimes they struggled with whether they needed more saddles or fewer bridles; whether to sacrifice the horse feed or to spend that money for a supply of horseshoes? Every change in the order form called for recalculating the weight and the budget, as they added or crossed items off their list or added them back again.

Some teachers might debate the appropriateness of this kind of exercise at the sixth grade level. However, of this one thing I'm confident; I could never have coaxed that amount of effort or commitment out of those girls any other way. It wasn't just a little math or a short bit of reading that made it so beneficial. It was the critical judgment and thinking that went with the problem solving, skills that we can talk about, but are very hard to teach. Someday soon, these kids were going to have to decide in their real lives how often they could eat out and still put gas in the car. Which was more important, a big wedding or a down payment on a condo? Sadly enough, we aren't very good at teaching these types of decision processes in school, and many young couples face real hardships in life because of their inexperience with critical thinking. Somehow, I would rather that they made plenty of mistakes and gain at least some insight into this sort of critical thinking from the Sears & Roebuck catalog, instead of waiting until they were in real life and doing it with their credit cards.

Another thing that made this type of exercise ideal was that everyone could attack the overall project from their own area of strength and choose their area of interest. In a world where no one can any longer be well versed in every area, people do the same thing in life. We tend to migrate to areas where we have natural abilities and innate skills. We no longer have the luxury of being able to educate each child in all areas. We must find a way to help that child find what he'd rather do more than anything else in the world, because that's where his special abilities will be. Choosing a career based on money alone is a concept that does not serve a person well.

Chapter 28

Henry Turns Cryptic and I Take Stock

Sometimes it doesn't hurt to watch your security vanish to keep you in touch with reality.

One afternoon after school, Henry appeared in my classroom with an unusual look on his face. With little greeting and no chitchat, he didn't beat around the bush and opened the dialogue with a statement that puzzled me.

"You know, Duane, you can't depend on always having me around here. You can't be sure I will always be here to run interference for you and our program. You should be thinking about what you are going to do with your life."

A little taken aback, I wasn't sure what to make of this. Was he tired of all the problems that the program and I created for him? He once told me that our program was the most exciting thing in the district, but caused him more problems than everything else put together. Or was he receiving more pressure from the principal or community again, to remove me?

More likely, he had finally figured out that I wasn't very good at what I was attempting to do. He had finally realized that I was just as much a misfit as most of the kids in my classroom. Or perhaps, he was just tired of it all and this was his way of saying to me, go get a real job.

Renegade Teacher

All that evening and part of the night, I lay in bed wondering what it all meant. By morning, I had reaffirmed in my mind that it was probably time for me to go back to the construction and apartment business I ran as a sideline, but where I was making ten times as much money. I probably wasn't being very effective with either, and may have been letting these kids down. Besides, there must be a better way to help these kids than in the hodge-podge, shotgun approach I was taking.

It was Henry's belief that if you are going to change a child, you will be changed in the process as well. He said it was that old law of physics; for every action there's an equal and opposite reaction, and that an effective teacher who really brings change in children will really be changed in the process. I didn't know how effective I was in anything I was doing, but in the process of my working with nearly 100 little girls and boys with all their problems, some of my edges had begun to wear off also.

No longer was I just arbitrarily angry at schools. I now realized that they faced a nearly impossible situation. I began to have a little more sympathy for the average teacher than when I had left high school. The children had given me a lot, and in return, I just hoped that I had given them at least something of value.

So in the morning, in the fresh light of day, I had come to a decision and went off to school with a light heart. This would be my last year of teaching. I would do the best I could until school was out, but then it was over.

Chapter 29

Henry Reveals All

Why is it that when hearing hoof beats in the night, thoughts of the Grim Reaper abound, when it just as well might be the King's messenger bringing us a sack of gold. —Unknown

The next afternoon Henry again came into my room after school and threw me another curve. He said, "I couldn't tell you yesterday what was really happening, but I can now. Last night, at a meeting of the Board of Directors of the new Community College they are going to build in Grants Pass, I was hired to begin the planning and construction."

He went on to say that he would be responsible for the planning from the beginning and had gone back into his little black book. He had pulled out the names of five mavericks he wanted to join him, and added that I was one of them.

Apparently the town of Grants Pass, about 40 miles north, had bought an old, surplus Job Corps site from the Federal Government. They wanted Henry to hire a staff to plan, and build from scratch, a new community college incorporating Henry's theories on better education techniques. This community college would be used to retrain the loggers and mill workers who were facing unemployment due to environmental pressures on the wood products industries.

The plan was to be up and running as soon as possible, using the old Job Corps buildings as classrooms until a new campus could be built, one building at a time. It seemed perfectly logical to Henry that we could build the entire campus with the students, teaching them all the various construction skills while we were "re-treading" them, as he liked to call it. Since there would be classes in all phases of construction and construction management, what a great "learning tool" building their own campus would be.

He continued by telling me how he, and five Mavericks he would talk into joining him, would be off on a great adventure. They were going to build a new kind of Community College, one based on "learning by doing"; how we would finally challenge the old Socratic model of teaching and introduce an experiential style of learning. We would have carte blanche to do the job the way we thought it should be done. No one else had been hired yet, and we would be free to hire whomever we thought was best qualified. Henry planned to build a most unusual community college, and I admit he did make it sound pretty exciting.

The key people in the community of Grants Pass had obviously been watching Henry and had looked into his philosophy on education. Apparently they even had visited many parts of the Phoenix School District. I knew that our strange little program had received a lot of visitors in the last year or so, and I knew they weren't coming to see me. Now I knew the rest of the story.

So that evening, I went home with my head spinning with possiblities. First, I was stunned at the validation that Henry was giving me. It continued to amaze me that he still saw something positive in this misfit. Second, there was a part of me that was really excited at the times when things would go right in the classroom. Was Henry right, was there really something happening with these kids? I hated to admit it, but I was spending more and more time thinking about "what might be possible" in schools, instead of "what was happening now."

Chapter 30

The Life Changing Decision

If the flap of a butterfly wing can alter weather patterns, then major decisions must be made with a faith in something greater than man.

As it turned out, I didn't go with Henry and help build his dream. It was a hard decision to make, but by this time my little construction company had grown. Ashland was a college community, and it seemed that all the new apartments one could build were full as soon as they were finished. So each summer for a few years, I had started building new apartments once school let out. By the time school started in the fall, the new ones were nearly finished. By Thanksgiving, all were rented.

This will always be one of the hardest decisions I would ever make. At the time, I felt it might have been a mistake, but in perfect hindsight, I now see its perfection. At the time, there were several factors to consider. One was that I would have to uproot my kids and wife. Then there was the monetary part of the equation, in that we would have to sell the apartments. Secondly, the quaint town of Ashland and what it was becoming had stolen our hearts and we knew it was the right place to raise our children. Being a theater town, it had just built what was to become a new award-winning indoor theater seating 650, to go with the outdoor Summer Theater seating another 1350. Ashland was fast becoming a year-round Mecca of the Arts and attracting many interesting people with small town values. They were people opting to leave the crowded metropolitan areas to resettle in this small town with world-class theater and old-fashioned values. This eclectic mix of people was instrumental in attracting good restaurants to go with its acclaimed theater. Also, there were the beginnings of what was to become a thriving wine industry. Added to all this, I was deeply involved with the community. I had been on the Chamber of Commerce Board of Directors for several years and was slated to be its next president. But, what about Teresa, and Mike, and Bobby, and...I didn't know.

"Smith" at home with one of his daughters.

Chapter 31

Scattering to the Four Winds

To every thing there is a season, and a time to every purpose under the heaven: A time to be born, and a time to die; a time to plant, and a time to pluck up that which is planted. —Ecclesiastes 3:1-2

It seemed that it was time for all of us to move on, to find that next stage of our lives; the kids, the teacher and the superintendent. The kids would take what they had learned and move into Junior High. Henry would go on to found Rogue Community College, the most innovative community college in America at the time as it probably still is today. The teacher would choose not to follow Henry on to the community college, but back to Ashland. There he would become part of the warp and woof of what was becoming one of the West Coast's centers for the arts and theater. Later, with his cat, Chester, he would build Lithia Hot Springs Resort, *www.LithiaSpringsResort.com*.

In the 40-some years after teaching, the kids he became so close to were never far from his mind. They would report back, keeping him informed of how they were doing. Teresa continued to show up on a somewhat regular basis two or three times a year. However, thirty years were to go by before he would know Teresa's real fate. But, something about Teresa continued to give him hope. He knew that, "when" a person showed up wasn't as important as "if" they showed up. Some people who wait thirty years to get started accomplish more in a few years than others accomplish in their lifetime. Someway, he wanted to believe that Teresa might turn out to be a mountain mover, or it was distinctly possible she might not even survive.

As for Henry, he was to go right on changing lives wherever he went. Those who worked with him always recognized his genius, but for Henry his rewards were the lives he changed. That meant more to him than accolades which he seemed to dodge wherever he could.

Henry is hired to build a new community college.

Chapter 32

Jan's Call from Florida

I keep thinking back to the class reunion. Who ever heard of a fifth grade having a 40-year class reunion? But then they didn't have a Jan Dunford in their fifth grade.

The class reunion idea had its start a couple of months prior to the event with a phone call from Jan Hook, née Dunford, one of my "kids." She spent two years with me, starting as a fifth-grader and managing to engineer her way into the next year also. At first she just called to say "hi" as the kids often did, and it was good to hear her voice. After talking for a while, she lamented that we hadn't seen each other for several years and how nice it would be to get together. I agreed, and after we chatted for a while about what she had been doing, we hung up.

In a day or two Jan called back and asked if I was going to be around in the next month or so. She then asked if she could fly out and visit. "Of course you can," I replied. "You're always welcome at the inn." Then she asked if I knew the whereabouts of a couple of her friends from the class. She said she hoped to see them too while she was here. After she got their phone numbers, we again hung up and I didn't think too much about it. Several days later, I got an e-mail from her saying she had located two or three of the other kids and was trying to reach others and would keep me posted.

Soon the list grew, and they started talking about having a reunion with their old grade school teacher. Soon, Jan was calling every few days and telling me who she had just located and how many she was in touch with. She asked how many the inn could hold for a reunion, wanting to know if they could hold it there. Since they were just planning to invite the one year of their own class, it seemed manageable and I told her it was fine with me.

Next, I was told to join Facebook and get a page of my own so that we could all catch up on the last four decades. Then the questions flew. They wanted to know about the class. One of the questions that came up was how the program had started in the first place. While they all had known Henry, the superintendent of the school district at the time, as kids they hadn't thought much about what role he played in our class and program.

When I told them we wouldn't have had a program at all if it hadn't been for Henry, it started another flood of questions. Soon they wanted Henry to come to the reunion so they could thank him personally for their year. I told them he had just lost his wife of over 60 years and then immediately came down with pneumonia. Though I doubted he would be able to come, I would ask.

While Henry was excited to hear that the kids wanted to get together and was touched they wanted him to there, he deferred. He had been sick for the last six weeks and didn't think he would be strong enough to attend, but he requested that he be kept informed.

They set a date in February and continued to make plans. Sometime in early January they sent out invitations to everyone they found. It began to look like this was really going to happen. Of course, Henry received an invitation and talked to me that evening, saying it was just as he thought. He wouldn't be well enough to attend. I knew he had taken the loss of his beloved wife very hard and, frankly, I wondered whether I would ever see him again.

Much to my surprise, less than a week before the reunion, I received a call from Henry saying he had been thinking about the reunion and wouldn't miss it for anything. His daughter heard about the invitation and volunteered to drive to the Portland area from her home in Southern Oregon and bring him back to Ashland. Thinking it might be less tiring, I invited Henry to come early and stay at the inn for a few days. We could spend a little time together and he wouldn't have to rush down and be back again. He loved the idea. Now I had something else to look forward to, spending a few days with Henry in addition to seeing the kids.

When Henry arrived, he looked like he'd lost quite a bit of weight, but he was in good spirits and said he hadn't felt so good in months. Henry was easy to have around the inn and the staff adored him. We ate our meals together and caught up on old times.

Jan flew in a couple of days early and joined us. She had a couple of wonderful kids and owned her own real estate company in Florida. In addition, she was active in the National Realtors Association and was slated in a couple of years to be the incoming president of a large Florida Realtors Association with 2500 members. Jan was doing just fine with her life and there was no telling where she would go in her life in the future. As a student, she had been a bit of a challenge because, being extremely bright, she could be a real handful when not challenged. But I never had to worry about Jan. It was a few of the other kids who were the cause of my sleepless nights. At the time, I had just made Jan one of my unofficial assistants in the class. She was part of the reason for getting as much done as we did.

The day before the actual event, several of the other kids joined us and preparations began. On the day of the affair, I was asked to take Henry and be gone for the day. I wondered what these characters had in mind, but Henry and I left without questioning them. When we returned that afternoon to the inn, they had closed off the restaurant and bar, and we were told to stay away until around six that evening. It was a beautiful day, so Henry and I enjoyed a fine glass of wine on the lawns out front of the inn.

When we finally arrived at the restaurant at 6:00 I was surprised to see both my daughters. They were toddlers during the era of this class; now they had brought all four of my grandchildren, who were busy staring at all the "old" people. In addition, there was a reporter from the local newspaper and someone from one of the local TV stations. I made the comment that this must be a slow news day in the valley, and one of them said they liked "man bites dog" stories. I never did figure out just what that meant.

Each year, the class was about 30 kids and they bonded very tightly. However, they didn't know kids from other years nearly as well, so this class only invited their classmates. However, after 40 years, seventeen showed up and many, of course, brought spouses. Many were from Oregon, with some from around the western states and some even further away like Jan.

With our old school room setting they had so faithfully created, it took us all back to another time and another place. As usual, the kids had hundreds of questions for Henry and me. It seems that as adults in their early 50s, they were very curious about things they hadn't thought about as children. This class was from the second year I taught, the class that became mouse farmers, raising white mice with all the unforeseen predicaments that followed.

The kids wanted to know why Henry had allowed our class to be so different and what started it all. Henry answered many questions that night and tears were shed on all sides. Some of the kids told us how that year had changed their lives. And, afterward, one boy, Randy, now a successful plumbing contractor, came up and handed me a piece of paper, saying, "If you ever write a book you can put this in it."

> *"When I got to Mr. Smith's sixth grade, I thought everything was impossible for me. By the end of that year, I thought nothing was. That was the only year I liked school and learned much of what I use in my business today."*
>
> Randy McCarty
> Medford, OR

Much of the evening touched me deeply, but sometimes I wondered whether they were all talking about the same class and year that I was remembering. Back then I had just been a kid myself, recovering from my own grade school trauma. As the teacher, I hadn't known at the time if what we were doing and trying in the class would ever be of any benefit to the kids. However, at the time, I rationalized it couldn't be any less relevant than many of my own experiences in school had been. So, in a way, I knew exactly what Randy was saying.

As the evening came to an end, we regretfully said our goodbyes and most of the kids left. Jan and a few others were staying over and we agreed to have breakfast together the next morning. Henry and I lingered for a while, not wanting the evening to end, and then we went to our cottages.

At breakfast the next day, Henry told us how this reunion had probably saved his life. He told us how sick with pneumonia he had been immediately after his wife's death and how he thought he would never get out of bed again, even questioning whether he really wanted to. Then he said, "It was the invitation from the kids which was placed on my nightstand that made the difference. It started working on me and now I am so glad it did. I am so happy to still be alive."

I thought to myself, "Well, kids, what a nice payback for all that Henry has given to us."

———————•———————

Find out what happened to the kids by visiting the author's follow-up books on Amazon.com (Search Duane F. Smith, Rebel Class).

Mike's Oaken Box Today

ABOUT THE AUTHOR

Duane F. Smith

Duane's unusual background and life experiences provide a unique perspective on traditional education, its potential and shortcomings. Having been born dyslexic, he found his own schooling a challenge and, barely finishing high school, left to join the Army. There he was to experience a life-changing event…teaching in an experimental program prepared for the Army by the University of Maryland. It left him convinced there was a better teaching method than the one-size-fits-all Socratic Model, ubiquitous to education.

After the Army he went to Ashland, Oregon and started renovating old houses as rentals. Meanwhile, in an attempt to understand why school had been so difficult for him, he enrolled in a psychology class at what is now Southern Oregon University, and one class led to another. Eventually, he received a Master's Degree, with an emphasis on early childhood development.

In his late 20s, on a challenge from a frustrated teacher he had met socially, he left an assistant to run the construction company, deciding to teach for a year or just long enough to test some of his new theories. Here he would meet Henry O. Pete, an extremely innovative school superintendent. They soon became united in their belief that the old Socratic method of teaching was no longer meeting the needs of students, teachers or society. Together, they developed an experimental program and put their theories into action in an actual classroom.

When, after five years, Henry was hired to found a Community College to be based on the same experimental theories, Duane left teaching to culminate his business career by building a unique inn in Ashland, Oregon. After two decades as an innkeeper, Duane, now retired, is writing extensively about his two favorite topics. **Renegade Teacher** is the first of several books related to early childhood development. Meanwhile, he is looking forward to writing more about the thriving restaurant and wine industries in Ashland, the once-rustic lumber town that is now a national center for live theater and the arts.

To follow what became of Teresa and the rest of the kids as well as the teacher and Henry the wily ol' superintendent, read the Author's new book:

Renegade Class
40 years after the original *'Renegade Teacher'*, you won't believe what became of the kids".. . . is now available on Amazon!

Printed in Great Britain
by Amazon